The Actor's Eye:

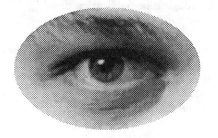

Seeing and Being Seen

A Fundamental Text

by

David Downs

APPLAUSE
NEW YORK • LONDON

An Applause Original
THE ACTOR'S EYE: Seeing and Being Seen
by David Downs

Library of Congress Cataloging-in-publication data:

Downs, David.
      The actor's eye : seeing and being seen / by David Downs.
          p.   cm.
      Includes bibliographical references.
      ISBN 1-55783-212-9
      1. Acting. 2. Krause, Alvina, d. 1981.   I. Title
PN2061.D68 1995
792'.028--dc20   95-34942
                                              CIP

British Library Cataloging-in-publication data:
A catalogue record for this book is available from the British Library.

Dedication

To Alvina Krause,
who taught me what teaching is
and what theatre can be.

Applause Theatre Books, Inc.

211 West 71st Street
New York, NY 10023
Phone: (212) 496-7511
Fax: (212) 721-2856

406 Vale Road
Tonbridge KENT TN9 1XR
Phone: 0732 357755
Fax: 0732 770219

Contents

Foreword

As the violinist has to learn to play the violin before he can learn to play Beethoven, so the actor has to learn to act before he can learn to act Shakespeare.

— Alvina Krause

The basic stages of actor training often fail to make the vital specific connections between the student's own life experience and the life experience at the heart of drama. Play texts need to be introduced in the early stages of actor training. Consequently, all of my illustrations of basic acting principles lead directly into plays: to characters from plays, to situations from plays, to significant moments in plays. I stop short of dealing with issues involved with memorized dialogue or the study of actual scenes from the plays in order to maintain focus on fundamental principles.

I urge actors to study life around them as a means of helping them to understand drama; to look at drama as rooted in real life. We shall see Hedda Gabler, not simply as a literary or theatrical problem to be solved on the stage, but as a human being as real as one own's best friend. We shall focus our attention on the world as a source of creative stimuli instead of focusing exclusively on ourselves as the source of creative response.

Students are encouraged to illustrate every idea in the book with active improvisational work as a means to discover motivated behavior as the essential creative medium of the actor. Chapter One deals with sensory response and the actor's ability to meaningfully perceive experience as a development of the histrionic capacity (See Francis Fergusson, *The Idea of a Theatre*). Chapter Two illustrates several aspects of human behavior and interaction that underpin much of drama: Response, Opposites, Relationships, Realizations and Decisions, Exits and Entrances. Chapter Three is aimed at developing an imagination that creates in an actor's terms. Chapter Four considers the factors that constitute human character and applies the work to the creation of character in drama. And Chapter Five discusses issues that carry throughout the book.

The plays most often referred to in the text are *The Sea Gull* and *The Cherry Orchard* of Anton Chekhov, Bernard Shaw's *Candida*, William Shakespeare's *Hamlet* and *Romeo and Juliet*, and Henrik Ibsen's *Hedda Gabler* and *Ghosts*. Other plays are referred to when appropriate: Chekhov's *Three Sisters*, Sophocles' *Antigone*, and Shakespeare's *Macbeth*. The chapter on characterization uses Edward Albee's *Who's Afraid of Virginia Woolf?*

The texts were chosen in part because of their likely availability in a student's library and the number of inexpensive editions offered by various publishers.

Introduction

"....the truth is, that in order to be a good player, there is required a greater share of genius, knowledge, and accomplishments, than for any one profession whatever; for this reason, that the profession of a player comprehends the whole system of human life."

— *James Boswell*

Psychological realism in acting evolved to satisfy the demands from such playwrights as Chekhov and Ibsen in their search for a new truth in their plays. Stanislavski augmented and clarified his ideas by observing great contemporary actors, such as Tomasso Salvini, and by studying the ensemble work of the Meininger theatre company. He primarily developed his unique methods, however, by grappling with his theatre company in their daily rehearsals. André Antoine and his actors in the Théâtre-Libre forged their new way by staging plays of Hauptmann, Turgenev, and Ibsen. In America, in the thirties, the Group Theatre developed ideas about acting while producing plays of social realism by such playwrights as Clifford Odets and Sidney Kingsley.

From the ranks of the Group Theatre arose the acting teachers Lee Strasberg, Stella Adler, Sanford Meisner and Robert Lewis, all of whom eventually opened their own studios independent from a producing theatre. At the same time, acting teaching began to flourish in university theatre departments; learning to act began to happen apart from the rehearsal work of theatre companies struggling to interpret and communicate specific plays of specific playwrights to the public. As learning to act became less and less connected to the production of specific plays, it began to focus increasingly on the actor and less on the playwright. (Perhaps the Group Theatre encouraged the separation when it began to feature its own in-house improvisations as public performances; the public became as fascinated with the process of actor-training as it was by the product, well-produced dramas.)

Much of contemporary actor training continues to focus on the primacy of the actor's individual self-explorations and revelations, often at the expense of the particular play the actor might be studying. When they are asked why they want to be actors, young people often say something like, "I have so much emotion in me to give," or, "I want to share my feelings with the world." Rarely do they say, "I love what Chekhov dramatizes about people," or, "I want to communicate the amazing vision Shakespeare has on life." In an interview in the Village Voice, "Silent Tongues," August 4, 1992, playwright and actor Sam Shepard said:

> "I think Strasberg ruined more actors than he helped....There is this whole kind of self-indulgent, neurotic belief that somehow the purpose for doing a play for these actors is to work out their private problems. They don't have the sense of serving the script. It's serving their own egos...unraveling their emotional problems...."

In an interview with American Theatre magazine (April 1986), Robert Lewis said, "When some Strasberg Method actors do Shakespeare at the Studio, they take Richard III and 'bring him to themselves.' I said to one of those actors once: 'Did you ever think of taking yourself to Richard III?'"

While these observations deal specifically with Lee Strasberg and the Method, the implicit criticism applies to acting teaching generally, perhaps because actor training in America has been so deeply influenced by Strasberg's Method. The emphasis such training places on the actor's so-called "gut response" to characters and dramatic situations, rather than on the expectations of plays and playwrights, encourages actors to think of characters simply as extensions of themselves and of plays as little more than structures through which they can share their emotions with a waiting audience. Plays and playwrights thus become necessary impediments to the more essential task of exploring, at worst, the individual actor's idiosyncrasies, and neuroses and, at best, what have become known as actors' choices.

The emphasis in current actor training on "truth to self" has become a limiting, rather than a liberating idea, as it takes all meaningfulness from the play and the playwright and puts it on the player. Most actors would say that they are, indeed, training themselves "to serve the play," but their training often does not teach them how to ask the play what it might want of them. They come to view their subjective responses to the play as identical with what the play dramatizes. Even as practical a book as Uta Hagen's *A Challenge for the Actor* keeps discussion of plays and characters separate from the work of actors on their creative capacities. The section of her book called "The Exercises" deals with one principle of human behavior after another without ever creating a direct illustrative and interpretive link to characters or actual moments from plays.

Artists need to ground themselves in solid principles, something enduring that they can count on. Actors are not taught to find such grounding in playwrights and their plays rooted in observable human behavior; they find it instead in their own subjective feelings, in their actors' egos. Recently I heard a respected teacher of acting say to her class, "To hell with the text, the play, the playwright. What I'm interested in is you. Are you connecting on stage? Is it real for you and is it real on your terms?" I had assumed that she was deliberately overstating her position so that she could put the actors' attention on the primacy of truthful response, after which she would surely emphasize truthfulness to the play and the playwright. But this same teacher carried her attitude into her own work as an actor. She was cast in a play by a well-known playwright who attended a week of rehearsals. When he suggested that what he had intended by a certain scene was different from the actress' ideas, she said, "Who cares what the playwright wants? It's what I'm feeling and whether it's real to me that counts. I'm the one who has to make it real."

During the run of the play there were performances when the actress' character was light and carefree, even funny; other nights she was self-pitying and lachrymose. Questioned by the stage manager about the inconsistencies, she said, "It all depends on how I'm feeling at the time of performance and on what I think about what's happening to these people at the time."

This whimsical attitude, unaccountable to any objective standard, is what can happen to theatre when the foundation of acting training shifts from the needs and expectations of plays and playwrights to the individual needs and neuroses of the eccentric actor.

• • •

Alvina Krause taught acting at Northwestern University from 1930 to 1963, and then in her private studio from 1971 until her death in 1981. Her own education had been anchored, not in theatre, but in the oral interpretation of literature, in platform performance and lectern readings of the kind for which Dickens and Wilde had become famous in America. She grounded her teaching, therefore, in the essential responsibility of interpreting and communicating to an audience the writer's ideas. When she came to teach acting, she naturally viewed it as the art one mastered in order to interpret appropriately and to communicate clearly the playwright's drama to an audience. While other approaches to teaching acting might have declared, "I want to teach you to act and, more's the pity, at some point I must use plays to do that", Alvina Krause's philosophy was, "I want to teach you to interpret and communicate the world's great drama and, wonder of wonders, in order to do that, you must learn to act."

Krause taught her students to first ask of a play, not "What is this about for me?" nor "How can I make this interesting?"; rather, "What does Shakespeare ask of his actors and what can I do to become that kind of actor?" or "Where in the world around me do I still find Moliere's concerns alive?" and "What life experience does Chekhov expect actors to bring to a creation of *The Cherry Orchard?*" From such fundamental questions the actor's more personal, individual questions follow. But for Krause these were not, "How does this make me feel?" nor "How would I react in this situation?"; rather, "Where in my experience do I go to find a Hamlet?" or "What part of me do I bring to my creation of Shaw's *Candida?*" and "How can I deepen and broaden my experience to meet the creative challenges posed by dramas and dramatists?"

Although Krause had read extensively in the literature on acting and readily incorporated its valuable ideas into her own work, she designed her classes and developed her teaching by working from plays to acting, not vice versa. She strove to discover what capacities theatre needs actors to develop before they begin tackling the great plays directly, and she learned to ask of plays themselves what they wanted from actors. What are the fundamental creative requirements for acting? What are the common elements behind all drama? What creative capacities do all playwrights expect of actors before those actors can develop the specific talents needed for specific playwrights? Such questions became the basis of the work in Krause's foundational acting course.

Krause certainly focused on the individual actor's creative self, but, unlike most training, she positioned the initial stages of learning in the broader and deeper context of great plays and playwrights. Her beginning students developed their individual capacities for truthful and insightful response, learning about themselves, their inner lives and their own emotional reserves. They did this in an environment that also asked them to look outside themselves for inspiration that connected discoveries about the self with discoveries about other people. This then led toward discoveries about dramatic characters and the plays of which they are a part. Krause found ways to directly relate situations of moment in the lives of her students to the plays they were studying; in turn, she connected characters, relationships and situations from plays to the private lives of her students.

I had barely started my study with Alvina Krause when I began a journal entry defining the objectives of the study of acting with these words: "I don't know how long all this will take...." She wrote above it, "A lifetime!" Those words were simultaneously discouraging and stimulating. Discouraging, because I was young enough to want to learn everything immediately; stimulating, because I wanted to devote my creative life to learning something that was, by its very nature, inexhaustible. I am no longer discouraged and each day stimulates anticipation anew: What will I learn today? What will the study of theatre bring to my comprehension of life? And how can I learn to perceive life more clearly so that it can illuminate my understanding of acting and theatre? And finally, how can I better communicate all of this to young people who want to learn, who want to soar, who want to become artists?

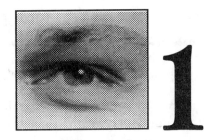

The
Thinking
Body

Before any understanding of acting, or any art, can exist, teachers and students must learn to use eyes, ears, all senses, to perceive, to understand in terms of immediate surroundings, to become aware of human beings; of the Hedda, the Macbeth, the Peer Gynt, sitting beside you.

— *Alvina Krause*

The Astonishment of Living

Years ago, as my mother was setting dinner plates at the table, she stopped abruptly, looked out the window and said with surprise, "My God, I helped drive your father out of this house." It was an astonishing moment of realization. In 1991, the little German town that had been the birthplace of my eighty-year-old Jewish neighbors invited 300 of its Jewish natives from all around the world to return for a week of atonement and reconciliation. After much soul-searching, my neighbors decided to go; they returned deeply gratified, even a bit conciliated. Astonishing.

Alvina Krause believed that an essential requirement for being a good playwright or actor was the desire to discover, and capacity to marvel at what makes people do the things they do. She called that capacity "the astonishment of living."

Harold Pinter revealed his capacity for such astonishment when he told of being enthralled by a man and a woman sitting in a pub, the man curious and sad, the woman tired and needful. "What," he began to wonder, "could have brought these two people to this point?" From that lone image, *Betrayal* developed.

We can imagine Shakespeare observing the loud, contagiously merry, fat man as he sits before the stone fireplace in the tavern telling his tales and playing practical jokes to the delight of all; or passing through a public square and watching a group of young men baiting one another, vibrantly entertained by their brilliant, mercurial leader; or reading contemporary romances and histories, and storing up the images and experiences that would enable him to realize a Falstaff, a Mercutio, an Antony, a Lady Macbeth. And Romeo leaves his friends and leaps over the orchard wall to explore the unknown. Astonishing.

Ibsen drew characters from life studies of the people he met and extracted plots from the newspaper stories he read. Hedda Gabler puts a bullet through her brain as her stupefied husband says, "Imagine that." The Judge adds, "But people don't do such things." Astonishing.

The good doctor, Anton Chekhov, filled his notebooks with character sketches of people he observed. Friends and acquaintances frequently recognized themselves in his plays and stories. Arkadina, the star personality, strides through the world of commercial theatre while her son shoots himself; the young Nina, eager to soar into a life in the theatre, realizes that what is important in life is simply learning how to endure. Astonishing.

The student of acting must become a student of life, alert to the astonishment of living at every moment. You can develop a disciplined capacity for astonishment and improve upon it for the rest of your life. And if you want to become a good actor you must start that process now.

Perception and the Senses

> *Oh Painter! You cannot be a good one if you are not the universal master of representing by your art every kind of form produced by nature. And this you will not know how to do if you do not see them, and retain them in your being. Hence as you go through the fields, turn your attention to various objects, and, in turn look now at this thing and now at that.... But do not do like some painters who..., though they see various objects around them, do not apprehend them; but even when they meet friends or relations and are saluted by them, although they see and hear them, take no more cognizance of them than if they had met so much empty air.*
>
> — *Leonardo Da Vinci (Notebooks.)*

> *It is an actor's passion to observe the world. It is his art to become what he observes. And finally it is his job to let the world observe him.*
>
> —*Richard Corliss,* (Time Magazine, *March 21, 1994)*

What, besides their expressive bodies and voices and their range of emotions, do actors bring to the creation of a Hedda Gabler or a Hamlet? Where in your own life do you uncover the capacities for response that can bring a Lopakhin to life? What have you experienced and observed that feeds your creation of Nina as she rushes around the lake to Treplev's little stage? Or of Macbeth as he waits to hear the bell signalling him to murder Duncan? Have you, as actors, seen, perceived and observed the Candida/Morell relationship so that your thinking bodies can understand that relationship and create it truthfully?

Ideas and psychological concepts describing behavior are not enough; actors must become students of actual human behavior.

The actor's creative medium is the total human being, and the fundamental artistic responsibility is the interpretation and communication of a playwright's drama to an audience. Much of Western theatre is founded on recognizably human characters finding themselves in situations that engage their deepest motivated selves in direct opposition to one another. It follows therefore that the actor who would learn how to interpret and communicate the widest range of drama must develop the ability to comprehend a play in terms of real people in truly recognizable circumstances doing comprehensibly real things. ("Real people" and "real things" need not be limited to what is usually meant by the particular reality of traditional Psychological Realism. Regardless of how theatrically unrealistic they may be, good plays are always rooted in perceivable reality; conversely, regardless of how realistic they are, good plays are always highly theatrical.)

It is through your sensory response to external stimuli that you learn about the world. And so it is with sensory response that this book begins. The more you study human life, the more you allow your senses to perceive behavioral motivation, the more deeply you absorb and retain these images, the more "creative raw material" your sensory and muscle imagination will have to draw upon, to bring humanity to the stage, to reveal the playwright's vision of the mystery of human life through theatre.

Develop your actor's capacity to experience and comprehend human behavior vividly, even when the human being is your own actor's self. Retain images of perceived response so that the sensory mechanism becomes a veritable storehouse of images with which to create. Trust the capacity for creative responses within yourself, but learn to explore the world at large for the creative stimuli you need. A simple analogy may help to illustrate: No amount of intellectual comprehension of what it takes to ride a bicycle, or conceptual description of how the body performs a waltz step, or verbal discussion of why a forehand shot must be executed in a certain way, will mean much to the person who wants to do these things unless, and until, the body discovers the purpose behind the precise behavior on its terms. Further, the capacity to perform the actions with comprehension resides within the person, but the stimuli to activate the body's understanding must come from outside the person: A parent shows you how to ride the bicycle, holds on to the bike as your body works to discover balance and motion; a teacher demonstrates the tennis forehand; you observe dancers as they waltz and you let your own body imitate, explore, and discover on its own terms.

Your initial attempts may be awkward, overly-conscious; the brain is in control of the body as it tries to use the body's muscles to figure out "how." The wonderful moment eventually arrives when the body comprehends not simply "how" to ride or dance or play tennis, but also the intricate muscular and sensory "why." You can now ride the bicycle without concentrating; you can dance all night long without thinking about it; you can handle the tennis racquet nonconsciously, concentrating on the goal beyond self, which is the rhythm of play, the scoring of points, the entire experience of playing tennis. (Consult *The Inner Game of Tennis*, W. Timothy Gallwey, Random House, 1974, for a beautiful description of how anyone can master a complex physical skill by simply learning to "let it happen.")

Observation must go beyond mere imitation and lead to sensory comprehension. We have all seen high school actors play the old persons' roles by imitating the walk, the voice, the little quirky gestures of the elderly; but there is no real understanding in the senses and the muscles, in "the thinking body", of the "why" of that observed behavior. Anyone can imitate, but true actors understand in every fibre of their being, the purpose behind behavior. Mikhail Baryshnikov has said that anyone can learn to dance how Prince Albrecht dances, but the great dancer knows why he must dance as he does. Baryshnikov meant that until the imitative "how" of behavior stimulates the "why" of bodily comprehension, behavior cannot become revelatory of character and drama.

In *A Challenge to the Actor*, Uta Hagen writes this about Paul Muni:

> ...his fanatic search for identification with his character was almost agonizing to watch. His background work occasionally went as far as going to live for weeks with families in the neighborhoods where his character might have lived, in order to

absorb, subjectively, the daily habits, the very atmosphere of his character's previous life." (p. 48)

In the March 21, 1994, issue of Time magazine, Richard Corliss describes how Daniel Day-Lewis prepares for each film by letting his body explore and experience. During the filming of *My Left Foot,* he stayed in his wheelchair even when not on camera, and he taught himself to paint with his foot. For *The Last of the Mohicans* he learned how to skin animals and shoot muskets. In New York for *The Age of Innocence,* he checked into his Victorian-style hotel as Newland Archer and wandered the city dressed in 1870 clothes. In preparation for the scene from *In the Name of the Father* where his character is battered into making a confession, he stayed awake for three nights, during which time director Jim Sheridan arranged to have him mock-interrogated by actual policemen.

Some of this may evoke the anecdote of Dustin Hoffman's staying up all night to prepare for a scene of exhaustion during the filming of *Marathon Man;* Laurence Olivier asked him why he didn't just try acting. But, even with excesses, the principle remains: You cannot act what your body totality has not experienced in some way. How we define "experience" is, in part, the subject of this book. It attempts to help actors become habitual observers and gatherers of human behavior (even their own). In the same way that they come to comprehend a dance step or a tennis swing, actors can perceive all behavior until it becomes second-nature, truly motivated, effortless.

We begin our consideration of sensory response by imagining an acting class of fifteen students held at Theatre Arts University. Each day, these individuals gather at a proscribed hour for acting class. They have things in common: They are all approximately the same age; they share contemporary cultural influences, such as music and fashion; they have lived through the collapse of the Soviet Union and the resurgence of ethnic rivalries in Eastern Europe; the struggle to expand the reach of civil rights in America; the effects of the AIDS epidemic on sexuality; the technological explosion that has created a world of communication and information-sharing unprecedented in human history. They may share similar social and economic backgrounds, perhaps religious influences. The unifying factor is that they have been drawn into the study of theatre.

For all their similarities, however, they each bring a unique background of experiences to every moment of life at the university.

No two of these people experience the same Theatre Arts U. No two respond in the same way to the stimuli in acting class. No two people perceive the same demonstration in the same way. Fifteen different lives, different lifetime experiences, different perceptions every moment.

Let's explore the implications of this idea in actor's terms. Each of the students writes quickly ten answers in noun form to the question: Who Am I?

For example,

Eva:

1. Student of Theatre
2. Sister of Terry
3. Challenger of Conventional Ethics
4. Daughter of Chris
5. Kentuckian
6. Roman Catholic
7. Friend of Tom
8. Lover of Dale
9. Champion Swimmer
10. Dog Owner

Eva illustrates "Daughter of Chris" by improvising in the most direct way possible in response to objects and environmental stimuli, not simply in conversation with a parent about illustrative matters. Perhaps Eva opens a care-package from home; Eva gets a letter from Chris, reads it, writes one in return; without undue reliance on dialogue, Eva engages in some experience with Chris that illustrates Eva the Daughter of Chris.

Eva chooses to present herself in her family's kitchen attempting to convince Chris to allow her to go to Northwestern University to study acting. While the situation requires a conversation, we only hear her side of it. What remains in memory are not the words, but the images of her sitting at the table playing nervously with an apple; lowering her head as she listens; moving to a corner of the room, hands hanging at her sides; several attempts to begin a sentence which are immediately squelched or sentences trailing off in a voice much less decisive than the student we all know as her eyes look up pleadingly or simply look at the floor. We learn a lot from those few minutes about Eva the daughter.

After the demonstration, the class analyzes: How does Eva the Daughter of Chris manifest herself in behavior? What did Eva's eyes reveal? Her voice? Her spine? As students isolate revelatory behavior, they demonstrate in order to discover whether their own muscles and senses have discovered and absorbed, or if only their intellect has been engaged. Jerry demonstrates specific responses that he thought were revelatory and the class analyzes his re-creation: What did Jerry truly embody? What behavior did he miss? Students go into action on the stage to illustrate their observations, to test their discoveries. In this way, actors learn to "discuss" an idea through spontaneous improvisational action; they learn to illustrate concepts through behavior; they compare ideas through actual human interaction.

Further avenues of exploration present themselves: What accounts for the differences among the various Evas? What specific stimuli most directly touch off each of these Evas? How does Eva the Daughter of Chris differ, in spine, in eyes, in use of hands, from Eva the Student of Theatre, whom the class already knows? Perhaps a friend in the class can demonstrate Eva the Roman Catholic and the class points out how this dimension of Eva manifests itself. Would Eva like to show us Eva the Challenger of Conventional Ethics?

Just as every human being has many dimensions within, so has every dramatic character, and just as the class worked to illustrate the principle with Eva the student, they can explore, as an example, Treplev from *The Sea Gull*.

Do the exercise, looking to the play to find guidelines for each aspect of Treplev:

1. Artist/poet
2. Son of Arkadina
3. One who loves Nina
4. Nephew and friend of Sorin
5. 19th-century Russian university drop-out
6. Son of a Kiev shopkeeper
7. Others?

Someone becomes Treplev as if he were a student in the acting class to illustrate any of the answers to the question, Who am I? Perhaps he chooses Treplev the Son of Arkadina. Let him write a letter from the farm to Arkadina who is on a tour of the provincial capitals. Or Arkadina arrives for her annual summer visit; he goes to the station to meet her. What present does she bring him? After dinner, he asks her to read his latest one-act play. Others contribute ideas. All follow the same process of analyzing and discovering as they did working with Eva. Come to discoveries about Treplev and about perceiving meaningful behavior, for understanding in muscles and senses, for determining stimuli that touch off the significant behavior.

If you analyze the character of someone you know, such as Eva, from this perspective, you can see that no one, however good an actor she may be, has in her own personal experience all the necessary components to create the complete character of Eva. Any one actor may have within her the capacity to create a truthful artistic characterization of Eva, but where does she go to find the stimuli and the experiences outside her that will activate the creative responses that can become an Eva? What experiences essential to Eva's make-up must each actor discover, experience, and store in honestly motivated behavior in order to become Eva the whole complex human being?

Similarly, the actor who would create Treplev may have great emotional reserves; in fact, all of the emotional capacity he will ever need for Treplev may be within him. And we expect that he has human experiences akin to the essential Treplev which he can draw upon to begin his creation. But no actor possesses all the traits, all the responses, all the life experiences, necessary to create Treplev as truly and fully as *The Sea Gull* needs him to be. As one obvious example, Treplev is a young Russian man of the nineteenth century and of a specific social class. How is an actor likely to have absorbed the implications for behavior of those facts? Where is an actor likely to find stimuli to metamorphose into such a person? Where will the actor who wishes to create Treplev go to find the several dimensions or selves that the play asks Treplev to embody? One of the goals of this book is to help answer these kinds of questions.

Note that this work is not yet the work of dramatic characterization, just as learning to ride a bicycle is not yet cycling, learning a waltz step is not yet dancing, learning the forehand is not yet playing tennis. No one who had worked to embody a capacity for response that was Eva's, or one of the traits of Eva, would say that she had created a full characterization of Eva. The same is true of Treplev. This exercise is designed simply to illustrate that keenly-developed senses and an ability to experience human behavior vividly and with comprehension are essential to the creative capacity of the proficient actor.

• • •

> *Living, the whole body carries its meaning and tells its own story, standing, sitting, walking, awake or asleep.*

—*Mabel Todd*, The Thinking Body

SPINE

....

We begin our consideration of the senses and the responsive human mechanism with the physiological center of the human being, the spine. In the way that a three-year old can be thought of as being a tantrum rather than as having a tantrum, the spine can be thought of as being motivation rather than simply as responding to motivation on an abstract, intellectual or emotional plane. Your spine literally embodies your attitude toward life. It literally embodies your relationships, your needs, attractions, repulsions, struggles, adjustments and adaptations, and becomes the motivational driving force of character.

In animal and human behavior, physical response begins in the spine, initiated by the large muscles of the lower back and the abdomen. To illustrate for yourself, observe a cat. Become the cat. Get down on all fours and let your spine become as flexible and as responsive as a cat's. Play with a rubber ball. Stalk a mouse. Get ready to pounce. Come to a sitting position and, with the muscles of the coccyx vertebrae, curl your tail around your body. Stand on all fours and curl the tail up over your back, whip the end of it back and forth.

When you are truly comfortable being a cat, repeat these activities in slow motion. Pay attention to what is happening in your spine. Note the aliveness and sensitivity of the muscles of the lower back and the abdomen and of the spine itself. The actor's spine should be as flexible and responsive as a cat's. Study a dancer's or an athlete's spine: the actor's spine should be at least as flexible and responsive, as strong and as sensitive.

You can learn much about the essential person by careful observation of his spine. Does the woman who runs the newsstand on the corner love her life? How can you tell from her spine alone? What is the attitude of your old next-door neighbor toward children? Let his spine tell you as it responds to neighborhood children. Let your spine respond to children as his does; observe him until your spine responds as naturally, effortlessly and with real comprehension.

Find a flexible, outgoing, responsive spine and study it closely. Let your spine lift with the delight of watching a frisbee tossed expertly across the beach; let it soar with the swelling gliding flight of a sea gull along the lake. Let your own spine discover the motivation of such an eager and life-affirming spine.

Look for a collapsed spine and a caved-in chest. Let your spine collapse, your chest sink. Avoid making an intellectual decision about how such a spine would probably respond or imposing a psychological reason on why such a spine behaves the way it does. If you give power to your analytical intellect, it will only force your body to do something pre-conceived, eliminating any chance of honest discovery in terms of muscles and senses. Simply let your own spine become comfortable with its new behavior. Let it respond. Let it discover that other spine as the central organizing feature of a responsive human totality. Let yourself respond freely as the other person until your own totality begins to understand why that person does what he does.

Let your spine come to its own conclusions about the motivation behind the behavior by following the process by which you learn to do a dance step effortlessly and with complete understanding. Keep the image of how you learned to ride a bicycle, or even how you learned to tie shoelaces: You observed and imitated, but your goal was to transcend imitation to true physical comprehension so that your body could respond without conscious thought. As you trained your body to dance and your fingers to tie bows, so you can give your spine the chance to respond as other spines respond.

Study your own spine to discover how it reveals who you are: forces are always at work on the spine, on balance, on equilibrium. They come in the form of external stimuli: people (What happens to your spine when your father enters a room?), objects (What response does your favorite childhood doll elicit in your spine?), music (What does your spine do when it hears the theme from *Star Wars?*), sounds (My spine still twists with a pang from childhood when I hear the bells of an ice cream truck), smells (Lilac takes me right back to my Grandmother's garden).

What stimuli lift your spine and help you to move forward in life freely, confidently? What forces strengthen your spine? What plays against your motivated spine? What can collapse it? Do you resist? In what kinds of situations? How successfully? Take the time to seek responses to these questions in active terms, not simply in contemplating the ideas. What forces, in terms of actual human interaction and behavior, play upon your spine?

I cherish the student who comes into my class from a high school with a minimal theatre program, whose vita pales in comparison to those who have lived their entire youths in theatre; the timid student who is convinced that others are so much more talented, so much more capable. The spine is attentive but stays in the background, easily cowed. Then the student gets to work, discoveries are made, in-class successes accumulate and the spine strengthens, begins to take an active leadership role.

I think of Jane, who, if she was thought of at all by her first-year classmates, was tolerated, but slightly patronized. Other students had instant responses to every question the teacher tossed out, but Jane worked undemonstratively. Her journal indicated that she was always ruminating on examples from class, seeking action illustrations in life and in plays, discovering her own examples, exploring her own ideas. She steadily worked to turn herself into an actor. Then came Greek tragedy. Jane was the first woman to tackle the gender issue as she worked on Agamemnon. The first in-class presentation showed an intellectual understanding that had not been fully translated into action. Agamemnon was passive, delicate, very much like Jane trying to act like a man. I was tough on her in class because I knew she always worked everything through until she understood it, and a week later she brought the scene back. It was terrific, and the transformation brought applause and some astonishment from the class. By the senior year, the class looked to Jane for illustrative work and saw her as a class leader. The delicate, shrinking spine of the insecure sophomore had transformed itself into the commanding, confident presence of an actress. Her spine told her story.

Look for specific spines. Look for the spine of the confidante. Whe.e are you most likely to find such a spine? What, in terms of concrete sensory stimuli, not in psychological generalizations, motivates it? Look for the manipulator's spine, the spine of the best friend, the over-achiever. With each discovery, let your own spine imitate, explore, draw conclusions. Let your spine discover: What if you were a doctor, a peasant, a couch   potato?

Put several objects or people in front of you: a child with a broken toy, a television set, a swimming pool, a robin in a bird-feeder. Let yourself respond to each with a mother's spine. Then respond as a rabbi, an accountant, a psychiatrist. And let yourself respond. See a child crying; let your mother's spine respond. Then the rabbi, and so on. See how your over-achiever's motivated spine or your psychiatrist responds to a television. Note the alteration in your responses to the same object as you become motivated with different spines. Look for such differences in the spines of people around you.

Look for the strength of the I-want-to-live motivation. What does I-want-to-live mean to your roommate? How does your roommate's spine manifest this motivating drive? What forces encourage, deflect, resist, distract? Why?

What motivates the president's spine? How is it manifested? What plays against it? Compare with the former president's spine.

Look for what plays directly against the basic motivating force of a person's spine. How strong is it? When does it win? Apply to yourself: What is most important to you in do-able, actable terms, not in psychological generalities? What external stimuli activate your strongest driving force as it manifests itself in your spine? Recreate it now. What force most directly opposes this drive? What desires or necessities play in direct opposition to this force? Be specific. Be courageous. What happens to your spine as it responds to these stimuli? Apply this knowledge to Treplev.

Student Joel tells of watching a family bring its laundry into a laundromat. The mother was tired and fat, her spine settled deep into her pelvis. She wore a faded house dress and her hair was pinned away from her face by a barrette. Her tiny eyes were studded in her pincushion face like two dull stones. The father blustered and huffed awkwardly about in a t-shirt and cover-alls, too big for the narrow aisles between the washing machines. Two sons, about three and four years old, accompanied them. The younger son raced about the room, screeching, getting into things, laughing, all of his energy outgoing and forward-looking, his spine lifted and alert, eager to experience each new stimulus. Mother and father offered occasional reprimands, even threats, which went unheeded and never materialized into punitive action. The older son sat motionless, shrinking. Each attempt to join in with his brother's activity was shouted down with threats. There was agony in his features, a tentative tremor in his voice. His spine was beaten down, slightly twisted. His arms fell at awkward angles, his hands fearfully gripping each other. Like a scolded and beaten pet, his entire body told his story, beginning with the spine and working into muscles, nerves, organs of sensory response. His attitude and motivation in life were all being formed in response to mother, father and brother.

Occupation

Focus on occupational spines. Perceive how the occupation of each of your parents has left its mark on their spines. Make an appointment to see the curator of a local museum or engage the librarian of your hometown library in a discussion about the rules of acquisitions. Study their spines. Go to a bank and try to get a loan and study the banker's spine. Study the spine of a pharmacist, the old man who directs traffic in front of the elementary school, the UPS person who comes to the door with a package, the head of archives at your school. Apply these to yourself: Let yourself do what the archivist does. Let your spine assume the behavior of that old man directing school children across the intersection, and let it do what he does until it responds as he responds, naturally, effortlessly, with total comprehension of the reason behind its behavior.

Observe Richard Daley of Chicago, Rudy Giuliani of New York City, or the mayor of your own home town. Election year is a terrific time to study closely and in detail the politician's spine. You will need it for Claudius from *Hamlet*, for Creon from *Antigone*.

(Creon must also incorporate the qualities of the statesman, perhaps even more so than the politician.) What is important to these spines? Explore, observe, study in specific terms. Let your thinking body come to conclusions. Avoid the purely intellectual, or psychological or emotional generalization: "All politicians are just fat cats who want the cream" or "Politicians are looking for ways to line their pockets." Even a more balanced observation is still too general: "The politician's spine wants people to trust it and believe it will do right by them." Come to the elemental "thinking body" motivation behind behavior. What, specifically, motivates the politician's spine?

If I had become a lawyer instead of a teacher, I would still be me, but I wouldn't be quite the same me: I would be me as a lawyer. My spine would manifest the difference, as would my eyes and my voice. Study lawyers' spines, eyes, and voices. Notice that if you don't know what a lawyer is, if you have never observed a lawyer closely, you cannot possibly

know what the effect that being one would have on who you are and how and why you respond. You must learn to store up life.

Apply to Drama

Let the plays themselves guide your work, let them suggest questions to you. Explore the characters' fears, compensations, contradictions, as they are expressed through the spine. Discover the specific stimuli of complementary opposing forces as well as the antagonistic forces at work on your spine.

The Sea Gull

In *The Sea Gull* Nina sees a gull swoop across the lake and her spine responds directly, freely, to it. In her muscles she becomes a sea gull soaring right to a pink cloud of theatre fame. Treplev sees the same gull and he, too, longs to fly freely, but opposing forces push down on him and prevent him from having such a free uplifted spine. Treplev is a vital, strong, young man who wants to live, to write, to create; but he is pulled down by doubts of his own capacities, by the strong forces of commercial theatre embodied in the play by Arkadina's self-centeredness (Improvise in terms of actual behavioral stimuli), by Trigorin's shallowness and success (Create in terms of detailed stimuli that Treplev must respond to), and by other influences (Is Nina alone in thinking his play is unproduceable?).

Treplev

Explore these questions in terms of improvisation and action, behavior and response: What is important to Treplev? What does he want to do? What motivates the artist's spine? Be careful of the intellectual verbal generalization: "The artist's spine is motivated by truth and beauty." Such a response is impossible to act and is therefore useless to the actor; put it into terms of specific stimuli and doable responses. The artist's spine perceives deeply, responds deeply, wants to communicate to others so that they leap to their feet in recognition, eyes wide open, as lightbulbs of discovery go off in their heads. What does "I-want-to-live" mean to Treplev in actable terms? How is that manifested in Treplev's spine? What process directly opposes this elemental driving force to do? What, as a young artist, does Treplev need that contradicts his artist's need to create, to communicate, to share with the world? What does he fear most? Express "That he may be a nobody" in specific terms and then improvise it, explore it in terms of action, of specific stimuli and specific response, until your spine comes to a full, effortless comprehension of Treplev's poet spine and its great fear. Why does he so desperately need his mother's approval? Manifest this in his spine.

Have you observed a Treplev poet spine in your experience? What does it want to do? What plays against it? If you set out to find that Treplev spine, would you be more likely to find it in a grocery store or a shopping mall, or an isolated spot by the lake at dusk? Why?

What turns you into a Treplev? What can activate your Treplev-artist spine? You-Treplev go to the lake. You watch a sea gull soar and circle; your spine lifts with the freedom of the flight. The sea gull dips and touches the mirror surface of the lake. At that moment a sunbeam streams through a cloud behind it and somewhere within your heart and spine you respond with pain at the beauty of the vision at something meaningful you sense contained in it all. Your artist-poet self wants to find a way to capture this moment, record it, communicate it. Always connect the desired response with the instigating stimuli; they must be inseparable. Let the outside world be the source of your creative stimuli for which you provide the creative responses.

Arkadina

Arkadina is a star, or, as she would have it, an actress. Have you stored up the Broadway or the Hollywood star spine? What motivates that spine? Have you perceived that spine? Where? Can you say to your spine, what if you were a star, if you craved applause, if you needed to be center stage all the time? (Why does Arkadina become short-tempered in the country?)

Does the sound of applause ringing through a theatre lift your spine? Do "bravos" shouted from the balcony give a lift to your ribcage and strengthen your spine? Does the sight of roses tossed at your feet, of your name on a program, someone asking for your autograph, directly activate your motivated spine? These stimuli add up to the motivation: I want to be a star. But you can't act "I-want-to-be-a-star." You can act "I want to hear applause and wave to fans in the balcony. I want to pick up roses tossed at my feet. I want people surrounding me asking for my autograph, pressing to hear stories about my life in the theatre."

Arkadina is 43 years old, but her actress spine resists gravity, fights aging. She looks into the front row during curtain call, sees a bald head, red cheeks, a carnation. She leans toward the rich old man: Objective? Get a diamond necklace sent to her dressing room. Her eyes lift to the balcony: Objective? Cheers, a rose tossed to her feet. Improvise until your spine responds naturally, habitually as the star actress, until you go past simple imitation and achieve true comprehension in spine, in muscles, in senses.

What plays against this fascination of theatre? What is the fear? Critics, boos, aging. Why is Treplev able to unleash Arkadina's fury in Act III? Arkadinas can be seen every night on TV talk shows, regularly on the Broadway stage. Are there potential Arkadinas in your immediate environment? Study them for clues.

Candida

Can you find something in yourself that reveals the Candida mother's spine? Once I asked student Martha, "What does 'mother' mean to you?" "A home and children," she said and immediately she looked at a rehearsal chair on the stage. Her spine lifted. A smile began to play at her lips. The rehearsal chair became an easy chair and as she arranged a pillow I stepped forward as a child. "School, mama." Instantly she smiled warmly, her spine turned to me. No need to "think how"; she simply let herself respond with her mother's spine, to me, the child. She leaned forward, her arms outstretched. "Come here, dear." I went forward. She buttoned my jacket, combed my hair aside with her hands. Her eyes smiled at me. She didn't try to "act like a mother"; she simply trusted her spine and her senses to respond. Martha had stored up the mother's motivations: the mother spine, muscles, eyes, and ears were absorbed deeply and vividly enough to let me, the child, activate them. She trusted herself to respond freely and naturally, to know her responses would be true. (What of the mother's spine does Mrs. Alving of Ghosts share with Candida? In Act III of *The Sea Gull* Treplev wants Arkadina the mother to respond to him, but he gets Arkadina the actress playing at mother. Try these two. See what you discover.)

In Candida there is also the teacher. The scene between her and James in Act II reveals Candida the wife becoming Candida the teacher. With Eugene at the beginning of Act III is Candida the teacher. She brings Eugene to a great realization just before Morell intrudes. Try these.

Notice I am still not talking about the creation of a full, complex character. Touching off Candida's mother spine and letting it respond is one device an actress will employ to create Candida, but it is not yet creating the total human being. That comes later. For now, we are concentrating on ways to develop your spine's capacity to perceive and to comprehend motivated behavior.

James Morell is a minister. What is the basic driving force of a minister? What does "to minister" mean in terms of literal behavior? How does the spine manifest I Want to Minister, I Want to See What People Need and I Want to Help Them, I Want to Bring Balance into the Lives of Others? Have you observed and stored up such a spine? How does Morell's spine manifest this force? Be specific: Take him to a shelter or to a hospital ward and let his minister's spine respond. Take him to an orphanage and let him inspect the kitchen, the laundry. He goes to a building sight for the poor where the construction foreman is using cheap wiring materials. Let him respond. Let yourself discover.

Morell goes to his library to find a quote for a sermon on marriage. In his study, Morell writes by dim firelight. What does Candida do when she comes in? Why? Note the mother's nurturing spine.

Why is it that Marchbanks is able to shake Morell's foundations so profoundly in the scene that ends Act I? Create the Marchbanks spine of his first entrance: ready to run in terror at any physical confrontation, hugging furniture, staying close to the wall. Then create the Marchbanks spine that takes his last exit. What has happened to the frightened spine that entered earlier? Locate throughout the play, and especially in the last scenes, the specific moments that change the Marchbanks Act I spine into the spine that exits into the night.

Varya

What specifically will you look for in the nun-like spine, Varya, from *The Cherry Orchard?* At one point, I was working as a janitor in a small Catholic elementary school that was in financial trouble. When fall classes started, the science lab would have to be closed; no one was certain how long the school could stay open. Sister Rosamund, the principal, managed the situation as firmly as she could. She had a straight, capable spine, eyes that faced life directly, a voice that commanded attention. But the strain was showing in an occasional clenched fist, a tense determination about the jaw, a slight red wateriness in the eyes.

Two weeks before school was to open, she came to me as I was washing windows in one of the classrooms. "Come with me," she said, her voice slightly quavering. She marched me with determination to the end of the hall, where she flung open the door to the janitor's closet. Inside was a metal pail in which an old mop had dried and rusted. "Look what the last janitor did," she said. She looked straight at me and burst into tears. "What am I going to do? What am I going to do?"

Part of me felt great compassion for Sister Rosamund who was a strong, capable woman of action; part of me wanted to laugh at the silly little thing that had set her off. The actor in me perceived and stored up: Sister Rosamund was Varya. Whenever I create Varya, part of me becomes Sister Rosamund pointing at the rusting mop as her school is falling apart and she is powerless to stop it.

How will you do the same to work on Nina? Describe how you might explore with Hedda and Lovborg. Discover Macbeth and Lady Macbeth this way. Give specific illustrations.

Gender

W. Ickes has defined masculinity "in terms of an active, controlling, and instrumental approach to social interaction" encompas16 16sing such qualities as "assertiveness, aggression, dominance, achievement orientation." Femininity is defined as "reactive, emotionally responsive, and expressive" as well as "compassionate, gentle, yielding, interpersonally oriented." (See Bibliography.) Recently, concerns about gender issues have permeated our lives. Since gender, too, expresses itself in spine, is there a gender-specific male or female spine? If so, what motivates each and what does each do in response? Look for illustrative examples, not just the obvious stereotypes. Look for the opposite, contradictory gender spine behavior, then ask what accounts for this variation to the norm.

How does "the Mother" in your father express itself? We tend to think of behavior that means "father": authoritarian, instructional, objective, reasoning, helping to survive in the outside world (Translate these adjectives into actual illustrative behavior). With "mother": nurturing, safe-guarding, emotional, inner strength building, etc. (Do the same for these adjectives.) This motivated behavior exists outside gender. What specific stimuli can touch off the mother spine within you and how does "mother" express itself in you regardless of your gender? (In class, Jane folds an old crocheted bedspread. Kyle discovers: "She's handling that with a mother's care!" Any stimulus can touch off any response.) In what situations, and in response to what stimuli, do you find yourself being "fatherly"?

Look at characters from Ibsen with regard to gender. Create the male-father spine of Torvald and the female-daughter spine of Nora from *A Doll House*. Compare the female spines of Aunt Julie and Hedda Gabler. Hedda has masculine impulses: she drinks like a man. Try it: Hedda lifts her glass in a toast. When she rides horses, she does not want to ride sidesaddle, though she is a Victorian lady. But does she straddle the horse? What is the implication for opposite forces in her spine?

Compare the female spines in Chekhov's *Three Sisters* with the male spines. Uncle Vanya might reveal interesting aspects from this point of view. Note in *The Cherry Orchard* that Lopakhin calls Gaev an old woman. Is there an implication here beyond gender to sexuality?

What happens in contemporary plays, especially those that focus on questioning socialized gender behavior? Caryl Churchill's *Cloud 9* is especially pertinent in this regard.

Nationality

Nationality is expressed in spine. Theatre Arts U. student Jerry tells of taking an overnight train from Geneva to Rome. At the Geneva train station, he was greeted by the uplifted, courteous, slightly aloof French-Swiss spine every step of the way. When he arrived in Rome, he was immediately accosted by a fast-talking, loose and flexible Italian spine. The man was trying to rent him a room in a hotel, but before he could respond another man stormed up and accused the first man of encroaching on his territory. They began to remonstrate, hands gesticulating and pushing as brochures went flying. Jerry backed away unnoticed. The flexible, responsive Italian spine, from which emerges the archetypal behavior patterns associated with the Italian language, was perfectly on display.

To perceive the nationality of spines, travel, or visit international airports, study films or find people from other countries at your school. Look for the erect, capable German spine; the settled-in-the-pelvis Russian peasant spine. Look at photos of Brezhnev and Khrushchev. What do they do that says "Russian peasant"? How do Gorbachev and Yeltsin manifest it?

Perhaps you have Irish grandparents. Discover how "Irishness" manifests itself in them. Demonstrate the Irish poet spine. In his *Time* essay, Richard Corliss describes the Irishness of actor Daniel Day-Lewis this way: "The tale-spinning, the mordant thoughtfulness, the smile in his soft voice that lightens his remarks with puckish irony." How does this description apply to the haunted Tyrones of Eugene O'Neill's plays? Find photographs of Bernard Shaw and Brian Friel. Discover the twinkling leprechaun present in the impish Irish sensibility.

Have you stored up the inflexibility of the "stiff-upper lip" English spine? What motivates it? Find clips of the royal response to the burning of Windsor castle, or the queen's speech about the "annus horribilis." Check television archives for video footage of Prince Charles responding to the man who fired at him a pistol containing blank cartridges.

Go to the Norwegian Embassy. Go to Chinatown. Go to a Russian Church.

What forces create the Manhattan spine? Contrast it with Los Angeles or the Pacific Northwest or the New England rural spine. What stimuli account for the representative Midwestern spine? Is there an urban African-American spine? Motivated by what specific stimuli? Perhaps you have African-American relatives from the rural South; contrast their spines with the urban spine.

Observe, perceive, and store up national spines in response to the stimuli that most clearly touch them off. Then apply this study to plays. What is this Russian soul at the heart of Chekhov? How do Noel Coward's British spines contrast Tom Stoppard's? Is there a Tennessee Williams Southern spine? Is there more than one "Southern spine"? Is the Mississippi Delta spine of *Cat on a Hot Tin Roof* the same as the New Orleans spine of *Streetcar?* Do some actor's research and discover the difference in terms of motivated, specific, illustrative behavior.

Observe how language rhythms, intonations, and sound values emerge from national and regional spines. Consider all of the abovementioned groups and discover how the language of each region or country is not only a logical outgrowth of the determining stimuli of the area, but also the vocal extension of spine, of physical rhythms, of the kinesthetic patterns inherent in each.

This does not mean to imply that all French people will manifest the same "French" spine. We are isolating traits in order to study them. When they interact together to create a total human being, they affect and modify one another, depending on what influences have shaped the whole.

Chekhov wrote that he spent the first thirty years of his life "squeezing out every drop of peasant blood from his veins." From photographic evidence, one of the manifestations of his Russian peasantness that he eliminated was the spine. His is a carefully-cultivated aristocratic spine. Did he eliminate all traces of the peasant? Compare photos of him and the young Tolstoy.

From a certain perspective, each of us is an example of many 'types' of human being. As a teacher, I fit into a type. As a middle-aged man, I am an example of a type. As a host, as a son, as a gardener, as a neighbor, I fit into types. What makes me an individual is why and how each type interacts with one another to shape the complete person. What stimuli touch off what responses, and which determine the total human being, who is me?

Truly motivated behavior can never be stereotypical, however much an "archetype" it may be. I once watched a man at a bar staring at a woman, while twirling the ends of his little pencil moustache. Shades of Snidley Whiplash, yet he was a real human being performing that "stereotypical" behavior. As I assumed his behavior and let myself respond, I discovered the motivation behind the behavior. My eyes focused clearly on the woman, the curve of her breasts, the way her hips moved on the stool. My eyes narrowed a little as I zeroed in on her physicality and my fingers absent-mindedly directed my energy toward her as they twirled the ends of my moustache. A satisfied smile crept onto my lips as my body grew more assured of its goal and its potential success. This was no longer just stereotyped behavior, but truly motivated response.

Always work in terms of specific details. Create the specific concrete stimuli and let your eyes, your spine, your feet, your heart, respond specifically. You will get into trouble if you think and work in generalities: "Treplev sees the lake" is too vague. Avoid trying to see anything in its entirety. We actually sense in details, in suggestive fragments. Look out there and see the sparkle of sun on the water. Is there a ripple from the wind? Did a fish just plop? These details add up to "lake." And let yourself respond.

The senses function like specific sensory extensions of the spine, especially in moments of heightened responsiveness: If you have ever walked alone down a street late at night, you know what it's like for your spine to hear the footsteps of someone coming up behind you.

• Toby Belch's (*Twelfth Night*) nose and tongue are olfactory extensions of his spine as he responds to Maria bringing a tray of cakes and ale.

• Gaev's fingertips are the touch extension of his spine as his hands reach toward the old family bookcase.

• Treplev's spine watches Arkadina in Act I during Nina's presentation of his play.

• Hedda's spine listens as Thea says she left her husband.

• Morell's spine hears Marchbanks firing sharply at him, "In her heart she despised him."

Develop the responsive flexible spine of the true actor. Perceive behavior vividly enough to re-create it on cue and with as complete and natural a comprehension as though you were born to it. Develop in yourself the capacity to follow through with a total body response. Dancers and athletes beautifully illustrate the primacy of the spine: the initiation of response through the muscles at the small of the back is allowed to travel through the spine and out to the limbs. By following through, they achieve the pointing of a foot or the flexing of a fingertip.

Let us now study each of the five senses in turn to learn how they can reveal the truth of human behavior to the perceptive actor.

SIGHT
....

The sense of sight responds to color, composition, movement, light and shadow, shape and line, among others. Which of these exactly strikes your eyes first? In my case, I see pattern and composition first. In my daily life, I am habitually struck by compositional patterns in my field of vision; when I first saw Vermeer's painting, "The Woman in Blue," I was struck by the geometry of it. The rectangular map in the right-hand corner, the flat tabletop, her spherical head and body, are almost abstract in pattern. Examine your own response to the painting. On the simplest level, what immediately strikes you about it? Ask yourself what this response reveals about you? I took in a short gasp of air, leaned back in my

Vermeer's *Women in Blue Reading a Letter*

chair, exhaled and slowly shook my head. A student of acting observing me might have discovered something about my sense of wonder at the craftsmanship of the geometry and the order. They might learn something about me by the way that wonder was expressed. (Organization in any form impresses me because I find it difficult to achieve.)

I always take in the whole before moving on to a revealing detail. When I enter a room, I stop at the doorway to get an overall picture of the situation before continuing in. Motivation? Fear, perhaps, not simply of the unknown, but fear of harm from the unknown. After I had leaned back in wonder at the craftsmanship of "The Woman in Blue" I plunged into the more realistic story details. The story-fantasizer in me was sent galloping by the hints in the painting.

Without thinking "how" for an instant, simply become yourself if you were a doctor. Avoid some abstract idea of a doctor, or thinking "what would a doctor see?"; this leads to manufactured and even stereotypical behavior. Simply let yourself become you-the-doctor and let yourself respond to the painting. This will probably involve more than just some internal mental shift of attitude; be free enough to make a complete change. If you-the-student are slouched in your chair, head leaning to one side, arms folded petulantly across your chest, then to become "you-the-doctor" will involve appropriate physical adjustments too. Trust your body, your totality, and let yourself respond.

What detail strikes you now that didn't strike you before? What response do you have? Be as specific as possible. Before, I simply recognized the Vermeer from an art history class; my spine straightened in satisfaction and I smiled. As the doctor, I saw the light on the woman's face and the curve of her spine and I realized she was pregnant. I was struck to my heart and my spine relaxed a little.

Become you-a-nun or you-the-painter or you-an-art historian. Your ability to simply and effortlessly do so depends upon what experience you have had of these people and what of their behavior you have perceived and stored up with comprehension. Early in my study with Alvina Krause, I had great difficulty working on Lopakhin from *The Cherry Orchard.* I simply could not create the man with any understanding, which puzzled me because I had grown up in a poor, working class environment of mostly Slavic peasant immigrants. In effect, I had spent the first ten years of my youth surrounded by Lopakhins. Why did he seem so foreign to me? Why was it impossible for me to create him with any truthful perception?

Slowly the answer revealed itself: I had spent my youth resenting the Lopakhins in my life. My senses had blocked out the experience; my muscles excluded my responses. I resisted storing them up so successfully that I refused to admit that there was anything like a Lopakhin living there. Consequently, I had to work very hard to recover these repressed images: Uncle Bill chopping wood and wiping his face with a red handkerchief; Uncle Duke waving his hands to punctuate stories of his life building the interstate highway, told in a loud, aggressive, unmodulated voice; my own father coming home from the steel mill and flinging his hard hat onto the porch swing.

Gradually my muscles and senses began to free themselves sufficiently to let me discover the Lopakhins I already had stored up within me, and to give me the impetus to go in search of more Lopakhins.

Studying Your Sense of Sight

Observe yourself in response to the stimuli of daily situations and ask yourself: What do my eyes tend to look for? What stimuli cause my eyes to open wide or turn away? Look for the response that reveals something about your inner self ("My eyes narrowed when I saw that woman slap her child and my heart twisted in pain") rather than the merely circumstantial ("My eyes narrowed because the sun is bright and I'm tired"). Ask the same questions of people you are studying from the point of view of their sense of sight.

What detail of a rose "catches your eye"? The shape? The withered edge of a petal? The deep blood color? What did you do in response? Did you look away? Were you pulled forward by the sight? Ask why you do what you do, what your responses reveal about you.

Let yourself instantly be you if you were your father and let yourself see with your father's eyes. This happens automatically to college students when their parents visit for the first time; suddenly the students see their rooms with their parents' eyes. Or your best friend from college comes home for spring break; suddenly you see your friend with your mother's eyes, or vice versa. You see details you hadn't noticed before, or you see them in a way you don't when you are just you. Do the same thing as simply and as effortlessly when you become your father and look at a rose. Ask what the alteration in your responses reveals.

Go for a walk through your hometown and become you-the-architect. What do you see? Turn a corner and become a photographer; then become the mayor. Let yourself see as a political refugee; not a generic refugee, that leads to stereotypical, false behavior, but if you were a refugee. If your muscles and your senses go blank at this suggestion, then they need to study real refugees in order to come to an understanding of who you-the-refugee might be. Perceiving the behavior of actual refugees will help you comprehend in muscles and nerves and senses who you would be if you were a refugee.

Some time ago, I was walking with a theatre lighting designer friend. The sky was aflame with the sunset; the sight stopped us both in our tracks. I saw a vaulting glow of reds and roses and ambers, and the shimmering light filling the air. My spine lifted, I tilted my head back, my chest expanded and a wave of adrenaline washed over me. "My God," was all my voice could muster. My friend's spine straightened, he tilted his head to the side and said in direct, businesslike tones, "Do you have any idea how much it would cost to light that?" What exactly did he see? What associations that are him did the details touch off? Instantly I let myself look back into the sky with the spine and the eyes of this lighting designer. I saw and responded to a different sunset. We are our responses, and, to perceptive observers, our responses reveal who we are.

Look at a sunset; now look at the same sunset as a poet, a nurse, a disabled person, your best friend's father, Elizabeth Taylor, Marchbanks. Note the difference in perspectives and responses to the same physical stimulus.

Specific Tasks

Set yourself daily actor's goals exercising the sense of sight. For instance, "Today I will go into the city and look for vibrant alive eyes that love to see the possibility in life." Where are you most likely to encounter such eyes? Let your eyes become like the ones you see. And remember: people look with their spines and their muscles, too. Study them. Let your own being discover motivation in sensory terms, in action terms. Try to locate such eyes in drama: perhaps they are Juliet's, or Irina's in Act I of *Three Sisters*.

Now look for a visually unresponsive person, perhaps the person across from you at dinner with the dead dull eyes. You look out the window at the autumn moon rising; your heart swells, your spine lifts, associations of crisp autumn walks with lovers play through you. The person next to you flatly observes, "Moon's up." No associations, no physical/emotional response. A simple and literal "Moon." Can you look out the window and see simply, "Moon's up" with no imaginative associations? Locate such people in drama. Perhaps the nurse from Romeo and Juliet, or Shamraev from *The Sea Gull*; certainly the rude mechanicals of *Midsummer-Night's Dream* share this literal response to life. Under what circumstances do you yourself see literally, unimaginatively, without associations?

Study a lawyer's response to life. Let your eyes do what her eyes do. See them narrow? What does she see in this particular moment that you do not see? Is it the lawyer in her who is looking? How will you know? Find out by letting yourself become her as easily as you let yourself become your mother to look at your room, or your father to look at the rose.

Avoid trying to see what you think you should see. Simply let your own eyes narrow, let them see what she sees, respond the way she responds. Note the changes in your usual perceptions and ask yourself, "What stimuli cause my eyes to narrow that way? Why?"

Where are you likely to see eyes in grief, eyes that have given up, or eyes that face reality head-on? Look for the eyes of a businessman, a politician, a dying woman, a spurned lover. Where are you likely to find each?

Study a photo of Chekhov. Can you simultaneously see the world with the deep compassion of the artist and the objectivity of the doctor as revealed in his eyes? What happens to your perceptions of the world around you when you assume Ibsen's eyes, with his monocle and his stern straight-on gaze, one eye magnified, the other narrowed? Let it happen. No need to impose any prejudiced intellectual conclusion on your efforts. What do Einstein's eyes reveal? Store them up with comprehension. Perhaps you will need them to create the blind Tiresias in Sophocles' *Antigone* and *Oedipus Rex*. Explore the implications of the military eyes of the World War II

Anton Chekhov   Albert Einstein

General Douglas MacArthur; they might stir something in you as you seek to understand Macbeth, or even Vershinin.

On her walk home from school, a colleague tells me that she passes a certain house every day. In her adult way she sees bushes and flowers in the corner of a yard (perhaps the apartment-dweller in her steels her muscles a bit against envy). She sees toys on a sidewalk and considers, as she steps over them, how somebody could trip and get hurt.

Recently, as she came past this house, she let herself become her-the-child. She didn't consciously think, "What would I see if I were a child?" or, "What is the right thing to see?" or, "I'll bet I'd see...." She simply let herself be a child and respond. Suddenly, the dark shadows under that lilac bush made her spine tense a little, as if preparing for a monster's attack; the hole beneath the stairs to the front porch caught her breath in momentary suspense; a particular turn in the stone walkway energized her muscles into exploring all the great hiding places in its shadowy underworld. Toys on the sidewalk instantly lifted her spine, her eyes smiled, her muscles jumped at possibility. She responded to external stimuli that activated the child she was.

Try the same exercise. What do you discover about yourself, about your response to stimuli, about your sense of perception?

Tomorrow, let yourself become a realtor looking at a house; then try a burglar casing the same house. Try a local celebrity, such as the mayor of your city. Note how your responses alter.

The Cherry Orchard

Let yourself become Gaev from *The Cherry Orchard;* the house becomes your family home, the toys yours and Lubov's when you were children. Throughout *The Cherry Orchard*, Lubov and Gaev escape from the pressing reality of the present into the carefree innocence of their childhood. (Lubov touches the little table in the nursery that was her favorite as a child; Gaev puts his fingertips against the bookcase that has stood against that wall for as long as he can remember.) They share their childhood memories as adults, smiling their charming smiles, innocently expecting the world to understand.

Test yourself: back in your room, can you vividly experience again as a child the house and the toys? Store up the details and faithfully recreate the experience. Now recreate the realtor's responses. The burglar's. Gaev's.

Trofimov goes to the cold, dark library where he sits and reads Karl Marx all night long by a solitary candle. He writes a pamphlet to be distributed around town. What happens to the eyes of such a person? What does he do when he discovers that he left the pamphlets somewhere and can't remember where?

Candida

Look for the eyes of the maternal Candida. Let Shaw help you to identify what exactly you will look for:

Candida...is looking at them with an amused maternal indulgence which is her characteristic expression....Candida's serene brow, courageous eyes, and well set mouth and chin signify largeness of mind and dignity of character.

Turn Shaw's description of Candida into motivated behavior: Let your roommate be a three-year old who can't quite tie his shoes; the mother in you/Candida responds. When Candida returns after spending the weekend with a sick relative, what does she automatically, even unconsciously, look for? Avoid answering intellectually. Simply do it and discover the answers. Come up the front stairs, open the door. Where do your eyes go immediately? Who will you look for first? Discover it. Experience it. Experience Candida's maternal eyes.

Try some further improvisations:

• Candida instructs the dressmaker about making her new winter coat.

• Candida enters the nursery; what does she see?

• Candida goes to the kitchen to slice onions. Let her help the cook.

• Candida enters Morell's office: James sits at his desk. Is the light bright enough? Is there wood for the fireplace? Are the inkwells filled? James' brow is wrinkled, he sighs. What does Candida see? What does she so in response?

Romeo and Juliet

Look for the eyes of Mercutio from *Romeo and Juliet*, alive to every stimulus; eyes that look for irony and paradox; eyes that shoot sparks as they twinkle and flash, revealing a lightning mind; images and metaphors peel off in more abundance than tongue could ever voice. Where will you find the eyes of Mercutio the poet, who has a profound vision and won't turn away from truth? In that young man in the town square with his friends? Be specific. In response to what circumstances do your friend's eyes become those of a Mercutio? Note how the vibrant, responsive body precedes brilliant moments of insight in his mind and on his tongue. When do your eyes reveal the Mercutio in you?

Search for the expectant youthful Juliet eyes, motivated to seek out every new experience life has to offer, to relish the astonishment of discovery through the sense of sight. What do Juliet's eyes see when she looks out from her balcony? Avoid the intellectual abstraction: "She sees freedom, youthful joy, etc." Rather, what does she literally see? Look up at your favorite constellation and let yourself literally reach for stars until you are standing on tip-toe, your spine alive to the possibilities that life has to offer. Look out over the garden and watch a ship with billowing sails come onto the horizon and sail into the dock of the city.

Run on tip-toe into the garden to greet your father, who brings a bundle of exotic new fabrics from the East. Run to meet Life, eyes open to any new experience. Illustrate, in behavioral terms, the concept that "Juliet is young, she loves freedom, she wants to live."

Juliet's nurse sees little. She aims for a comfortable chair by the fire, an empty bench to put up her feet in the shade to escape the hot Verona sun. Improvise these responses until they come naturally. Go on an errand and see a rich young man; there's shade on the road, your feet ache from walking. It's hot, and the wimple makes you sweat. Your stomach rumbles: "Have they eaten that beef stew at home yet? Will the big chair in the kitchen be empty?" Improvise until you are responding with the Nurse's old eyes, the Nurse's adult needs.

Where are you likely to find a person with such eyes? In my experience, Nurse personalities make their way to the elevated train platforms at the end of a day spent housekeeping in the suburbs. Their swollen hands grip stuffed shopping bags as they trudge up the stairs. They grab hold of the railing and grunt a bit when they pull themselves up. When they come onto the platform, their eyes search for an empty seat on one of the passenger benches. When they see one, Ah! a slight smile passes across their face and they lumber toward it, muscles anticipating how good it will feel when they can give in to gravity and settle onto the seat.

What is most important to the Nurse? What does she see when she looks at Juliet? What specific sensory stimuli (not generalizations, like "She sees her young mistress") evince her literal response? What does the Nurse fail to see? Perhaps you have an elderly aunt or a grandmother who loves you, but whose aching bones would not surprisingly rather sit comfortably on the porch swing than run an errand to your boyfriend's house. Let your work lead to the essential role the Nurse plays in the inevitable tragedy of Romeo and Juliet.

Allow yourself to respond with your stored-up research. Similarly, you must be free to change as new stored-up responses accumulate. Develop the artist's ability to discriminate meaningful responses and to store them up for creative use later. Freedom to respond coupled with true sensory perception is the goal.

HEARING

Our sense of hearing responds to pitch, range, rate, volume, and intensity. Our ears tell us where we are in the world; the directions from which sounds emanate and the distance between us and the sound sources give us our 360°, three-dimensional sense of environment. Hearing is largely responsible for our orientation in space. In her book, *Listening* (New York: Harper Collins, 1994), Hannah Merker writes, "Psychologists say that deafness, or a severe hearing loss, acquired after a human being has known hearing, can be the single greatest trauma a person can experience." Taking a walk with ears plugged through even the most familiar neighborhood can be a most instructive exercise.

Turn out the lights and have someone activate a variety of sound-making devices one by one. Let yourself respond vividly to the sound: a cow bell, a dinner bell, a door bell. A vase smashes against a wall. Try different kinds of knocks on a door, a tapping sound, a grating sound. Try a scratch, a scuffling sound; blow across the open mouths of various bottles. Take note of your literal responses in the same way you did when study.ing the sense of sight: What did you hear? What associations did you make? What do your responses reveal about you?

Study your aural response to life: Which quality of sound do you respond to most immediately? When is volume more meaning-ful than pitch? In what circumstances are you unaware of sound? When is the sense of hearing more significant than the sense of sight? Do you know someone who responds with a keener sense of hearing than sight? Following the guidelines for visual response to Vermeer's painting, "Woman in Blue," discover what you fail to hear in each sound stimulus by letting yourself become other people. Respond to the same sound as a librarian, your mother, a well-known politician, Prossy Garnett in *Candida*. Describe the differences in your responses each time. What if you were a composer, a hiker, or James Morell? When Macbeth hears knocks at the door (II, ii), what do they sound like? How much time lapses between knocks? Why?

Respond to a contemporary song. Immediately listen again as your father. Respond now as a DJ, then as Frank Sinatra, or Jesse Helms, or Bart Simpson. What alterations in your hearing, your responses, your perceptions accompany each transformation?

We hear not only a particular sound but whatever experi-ences we bring to that sound. Listening to a song that was popular at some earlier period in your life may touch off vivid associations and responses. These are not simply mental images or abstract memories, but actual re-lived experiences, however instantaneous that re-living is.

Note the way sound touches off associations in each person's character. Choose stimuli that logically apply to characters from plays. Play a Chopin waltz:

• Treplev from *The Sea Gull*, tosses stones into the lake. Perhaps he is arrested by the sound mid-toss; perhaps something deep in his heart swells as he watches ripples move out into the lake.

• Masha, standing in the window of an upstairs room as she watches Treplev, listens to the waltz. Somewhere inside the part of her she tries to stifle with drink something stirs. Perhaps she sways as her fingers touch the curtain.

• Arkadina, dressing for lunch, hears the waltz in the distance. Perhaps she lightly strokes her hair, and gazes into the mirror. What does she see? And does she immediately lift her spine and a give girlish swirl of her skirt?

Each hears something different and each does something different, something characteristic, in response. Let yourself explore and discover by actual experience.

Become Mercutio and hear a rowdy drinking song. Now hear the same song as the Friar; then Lord Montague; the Prince. Discover how human beings reveal who they are through their responses to stimuli. Avoid deciding what each would do and then making yourself do that. Simply let yourself respond and discover.

Hearing and the Human Voice

Human beings most often respond to the qualities of the human voice than to the literal words being spoken. Test yourself: let voices play on your inner ear and spine. What tones soothe? What happens to you in response? What tones grate, seduce, encourage, repel? What quality lulls? What stimulates? What intonations jab at your spine, tickle it, stiffen it? What do you actually hear? In response to any aural stimulus ask: To what specifically am I responding? What associations are touched off? Why? Discover what you fail to hear by instantly becoming a minister, a waiter, a doctor, a child, a police officer.

Learn to hear with your whole body, not just your ears.

Listen for dry voices, voices that cajole, for musical voices that run up and down the scale, for dead voices and monotones. What has caused the specific details that you sense? What does your friend's voice reveal about him? Have you stored up your employer's vocal responses to life? What have you learned about her through hearing? What did that person's voice reveal as he described his father's recent illness? Can you recreate these responses with understanding?

Listen to the person sitting next to you: perceive pitch, tempo, volume, range. Get to the source, the motivation of such voices. Ask why this person speaks so loudly. Avoid the judgmental stance: "This person is a jerk who just wants attention." Rather, adopt a position of understanding, ask the question from the person's point of view and discover the motivation. Let your own voice explore: What if I stated facts in the blunt, unmodulated tones of that person? What if my voice automatically came out loud and ended each statement with a BANG? Work until your own body understands the motivation and can speak naturally, habitually with such a voice. Apply your discoveries to Shamraev of *The Sea Gull* as he waxes enthusiastic about seeing Duse. Or to Lopakhin from *The Cherry Orchard* broaching the subject of subdividing the estate as he catches up with Lubov and Gaev on a walk into the orchard. Or Solyony in *Three Sisters* as he tells Irina that he loves her.

Laughter

Listen to laughter. Note where in the body, in the whole human being, a laugh originates. Some people seem to laugh from their hearts, some from their guts. Others seem to laugh from a dry removed place. Some laugh with no humor at all; where do their laughs come from? Recreate that laugh coming from the person behind you that sends chills up your spine. Let your own ears and muscles and vocal mechanism discover where such a cold laugh comes from, and say, "Yes, I can laugh this way with real sensory understanding of what motivates it." In doing so, what do you discover about the person who produced the laugh?

Yasha from *The Cherry Orchard* laughs at Dunyasha and at Fiers. In response to what stimuli does he laugh? What kind of a laugh is it? Let the play lead you. Describe his laugh. Be specific.

What motivates it? How will you know when you have heard the Yasha laugh in real life?

Where does Hedda's laugh originate? What does the laugh sound like of a person who faces directly, and with mordant irony, the reality that she is trapped and being stifled by even the most trivial stimuli (Tesman sniffs his collection of old books, Aunt Julie clucks over Hedda's wedding ring)?

What does Richard III's laugh reveal about himself after his successfully wooing of Lady Anne?

The Sea Gull

Arkadina is a nineteenth-century stage star. Her seductive voice is trained in elocution, well-modulated, capable of lifting effortlessly to the last row of the balcony. The exquisite range, the liquid melody playing up and down the scale, delights, invites, charms. And the motivation? Arkadina must be the center of attention, must have people sitting at her feet. What do other people do in response to such an enchanting voice? Try it. Explore. Discover Arkadina through her voice.

Create a characterization of Trigorin from voice alone. Have you heard the dried-up Trigorin voice on television talk shows coming from an actor or writer who has long since sold out? With his dry, tight voice he says, "This next role is just perfect, I think this movie really has some important things to say." Can you intuit, beyond intellect and words, the motivation behind such a voice?

Search for a Nina voice, an untrained but beautiful, naturally lyrical voice, astonished by the very presence of a star actress, of a famous writer. If the actress you admire most and a famous writer were to visit your school tomorrow and wanted to see you perform.... Let yourself respond. Let yourself do what you would do. What happens to your eyes, your voice, your spine?

Explore:

• Arkadina hears undertones in Trigorin's compliment to Nina after Treplev's play in Act I. What does she have an impulse to do?

• Polina hears the silence after Shamraev kills conversation with one of his stories, told in his loud, thumping, unmodulated voice. She nearly bursts into tears of humiliation and rage. What does she do instead? With what effect on her voice?

• Arkadina wants to persuade Sorin to stay at home and not come with her to town. What happens to her voice? Why does she not want Sorin to be seen with her?

Hedda Gabler

Hedda hears Tesman's pattering footsteps. Aunt Julie fusses over Hedda's morning dress. What exactly does Aunt Julie's voice do to Hedda's spine? What does Aunt Julie hear in Hedda's voice? How does Lovborg's voice reveal the poet? What qualities does Brack's man-on-top-of-the-world voice possess? Contrast with Tesman the researcher, Tesman the nephew, Tesman the host. Avoid the easy intellectual answer, and let yourself become each of these and respond truthfully. Explore and discover illustrations from life.

Candida

Candida sees James working late, sees his hand lift to his eyes, and part of her response is vocal. What motivates and reveals "concerned mother" in voice? Prossy has eliminated gentle tones from her voice, eliminated resonance, liquid vowels. Why? Set yourself the task of finding the Prossy voice: dry, business-like, practical, unrevealing. (Turn these adjectives into actual motivated, revelatory behavior.) She stifles any heartfelt response before it can find vocal expression, until Marchbanks, at the beginning of Act II, sees through the external stereotype to the human being beneath. Let yourself do it and discover. What do you discover about Marchbanks in the process?

Pot Pourri

• Each of the summer party people in Act I of *The Sea Gull* hears the music from across the lake. To what private experience or recollection does each drift? What does the recollection tell you about the character?

• The group in Act II of *The Cherry Orchard* hears the string-snapping sound in the distance. But what does each character actually hear? How do each of them react?

• What changes in Juliet's character are signaled by changes in her voice from, "The clock struck nine when I did send the nurse..." to, "Gallop apace, you fiery-footed steeds..." to, "Ancient damnation! O most wicked fiend..." when she hears the nurse tell her to marry Paris?

• What happens to the character of Nora Helmer's voice from the first act of *A Doll House* to the end of the play? How? Why? Be specific.

• Nina delivers the lines from Treplev's play in Act I and then again in Act IV. What has happened to her and to her voice between the two? What is the drama? The irony?

• Note the changes in Irina's voice through all four acts of *Three Sisters.*

Look for gender manifestations of voice:

• Hedda is an educated woman in nineteenth-century Norway. Compare her voice with Thea's, with Berthe's, with Aunt Julie's.

• Gaev, that "silly old woman," as Lopakhin once says, addresses the bookcase. What does his voice reveal besides "silly old woman"?

• What is "masculine" about the voice of Juliet's Nurse? Are there gender assumptions in classic dramas expressed in voice that contemporary dramaturgy has exploded? What does the actor playing Betty in *Cloud 9* reveal through his voice? Why? What are the implications?

TOUCH

Do you respond to the world with a vibrant sense of touch? Do you experience textures and shapes? Do you find yourself touching people and objects in the world? If yes, how do you touch them? What does that habit reveal about you? If no, what do your hands do, and what does that reveal about you? To what does your sense of touch respond? To what touch stimuli does your spine follow through?

Select a book to which you have a vivid response. Perhaps you love Jane Austen and you locate an early edition of *Pride and Prejudice*; perhaps as a child you were particularly fond of *The Velveteen Rabbit*, or *James and the Giant Peach*. Choose that one from the shelf. Let yourself respond to it. What do we learn about you from the way you respond to the book? To its jacket, its illustrations, the binding, the paper? Let someone else recreate your responses.

Using the same book, respond to it as a cookbook, then an encyclopedia, an address book, your best friend's diary. Note how different your responses to its physical features are each time.

Become you-the-librarian and respond to the book; then, you-the-mother; the illiterate; the blind person; the immigrant who does not speak the language.

Take a controversial book such as *Heather Has Two Mommies*. Turn yourself into an interesting contemporary person and let him or her read the book. Then become Candida and open the book. Try Pastor Manders *(Ghosts)* or Falstaff. Record your discoveries in your journal.

• Improvise Candida bringing James his Bible. Then do it as James.

• Let someone hand you-Arkadina one of Trigorin's books; then a magazine with one of Treplev's recently-published stories; then let yourself pick up the script of the play you-Arkadina will star in next season.

• Lopakhin chooses a book of poetry from Gaev's bookcase as he waits for Lubov to arrive at the beginning of the play.

• Mrs. Alving *(Ghosts)* reads one of Wollstonecraft's book on women's rights. Pastor Manders takes his Bible from its place; then, he picks up Mrs. Alving's book and opens it. Let Regina pick up the book as she dusts. Then she sees a travel brochure.

Use easy simple direct characteristic behavior. What does the sense of touch reveal about each of these characters? How is motivation expressed in their hands? What do you discover about each by exploring with the sense of touch?

Explore the following:

• Lubov goes to a dress shop in Paris.

- Oswald touches a piece of cherry-colored velvet.

- Morell puts on his coat.

- Lopakhin puts on his coat.

- Marchbanks puts on his coat.

- Romeo chooses a rapier.

- Tybalt chooses a rapier.

- Macbeth wields a broadsword on the open battlefield.

- Macbeth unsheaths a dagger in the castle.

- Invent other possibilities; improvise and discover, then record your discoveries in your daily journal.

Study hands

What can you discover about people from hands alone? Start, as always, with yourself: what do your hands reveal about you? What do they do that reveals your age, your gender? Be specific. How, by their behavior, not just their appearance, do your hands express nationality? Occupation? Social class? Demonstrate in terms of specific details of behavior, of actual response to specific stimuli. What would a perceptive person discover through your hands about your emotional condition, about your attitude toward manual labor? What about you-the-teacher, you-the-actor, the reader, the parent?

Observe several doctors. A half-hour's research in the waiting room of a clinic should suffice. How do a doctor's hands reveal "doctor"? Let your own hands respond and discover. Become you-the-doctor. What is the difference between you-the-doctor and the current you? What alterations are there in response between the two? Why? What do male and female doctors share in their hands and sense of touch that is "doctor," regardless of gender differences?

There is no suggestion here that there is a "right" response. Indeed, all people who turn themselves into doctors will not by any means have the same "right" response. The point is: you if you were a doctor. Will Dr. Dorn (*The Sea Gull*) and Dr. Astrov (*Uncle Vanya*) and Dr. Chebyutikin (*Three Sisters*) share something in the way their hands respond to the world? Will there not be, in all true doctors, a common "doctorness" expressed in hands and the sense of touch?

Will it be exactly the same for all three? What kind of a doctor is Dorn? What type is Chebyutikin? John Buchanan in Tennessee Williams' *Summer and Smoke*?

Watch hands at a construction site: Lift a cinder block, carry it, put it down; push the hard hat back, light a cigarette. Then apply these active observations to Lopakhin (heft an axe, chop a tree, toss a log onto a pile); Shamraev (hitch a horse to a hay wagon, cuff one of the fieldhands, pull your boots on in the morning); Juliet's nurse (peel an apple, drink a beer, test the cushion on the chair to see if it's soft).

How can you tell which hands belong to a college student working construction for the summer?

Study a violinist's hands (Note the opposition and drama in Itzhak Perlman). Study a bricklayer. Look for hands with arthritis. Look at the hands of a blind person. Take note of old expressive hands: Watch the tape of Vladimir Horowitz playing in Moscow. In each case, let your own hands do what they see the other's hands doing. Let your own hands explore, perceive, respond.

As you study other people's responses, ask yourself: When do I respond like that? If I don't reach for a cigarette at this kind of moment, what do I do? Why? What could turn my hands into hands like those of the person next to me?

Look for opposites:

•Perhaps the construction-site hands turn around and handle a baby delicately and lovingly. Can you locate such hands in drama? Perhaps Joe Bonaparte in Clifford Odets' *Golden Boy*.

•Or perhaps they can't. My Uncle Duke spent his working life greasing the machinery on the vehicles that built the American toll roads in the fifties. His hands worked as single units, like big paws. He could not pick up something as tiny as a dime: Shamraev? Lopakhin? (Trofimov says to him in Act IV, "You have the hands of a poet.")

•Mary Tyrone's arthritic hands in *Long Day's Journey* want to play Brahms on the piano.

•Candida's hands seem like a Madonna's hands to Marchbanks, yet they peel onions in the scullery and trim the wicks on the lamps for the house.

Study the language of hands: farmer's hands, mother's hands, expressive artistic hands, hands that work outdoors. (Among the complaints that The New Republic film critic Stanley Kaufmann had about the remake of *Of Mice and Men* was that John Malkovich, as Lenny, simply did not have hands that did manual labor.) Study the hands of a bankteller, a policeman, a Caucasian-American jeweller, a Japanese business person, a Russian politician, a Native American lobbyist.

Study three florists or bakers or receptionists. Is there something about the hands of all three that says "florist," "baker," "receptionist," even as each person is a unique individual? Can your hands then do a florist, a baker, a receptionist? As you study, the objective is to discover "why," to let your thinking body and your thinking senses get to the motivation behind human behavior.

When do your hands reveal something other than what your eyes and voice are communicating? Hands and feet always express the unspoken preoccupations. For example, the fingers rip at a styrofoam cup as the person across from you tells you that he is perfectly happy in his domestic situation. Or the foot taps impatiently while the eyes say "I am enjoying myself." Apply this idea to Masha and Trigorin at the beginning of Act II of *The Sea Gull*. Study this in yourself and in others. Look for subtle illustrations.

What influence has socialized gender behavior had on your hands? Be specific. Study young hands being trained to be a woman's hands, a man's hands. Note the effect of social and economic status on such behavioral development. Look for hands that defy the gender role. Look for the why behind it.

Apply to characters in drama:

• As Lubov takes coins from her little purse, they slip through her fingers.

• Varya pins up Anya's hair and Anya lets the pins slip through her fingers, too. Like mother, like daughter.

• Hedda Gabler's Victorian lady's hands lift, aim, and shoot a pistol.

• How do Burgess' hands compare to Marchbanks'?

• Shamraev's to Treplev's?

- Gaev touches the bookcase, reaches for a candy as Lopakhin takes a delicate book of poetry out of the bookcase.

- Develop more illustrations.

Try Comparative Studies

One day we hold class in the dance rehearsal room instead of the usual theatre. The curtain is up at the barre and the mirrors revealed, but I want to drop the curtain. I walk over to the pulley system, but confronted with an unfamiliar mechanical problem, my hands suddenly go limp; they hang helpless and ineffectual. I turn immediately to the class, my hands lifted in supplication. "Does someone know how to work this?"

Let your hands come to their own understanding of the "why" behind the behavior of my hands and let them respond to the pulley automatically, unconsciously, with the same motivation as my hands. The "why" of the hands is to seek help. They fall limp when confronted with technical tools. It's rather unlikely that you have ever met me or seen me. But you need not know me or my biographical "why," in order for your hands to understand in their terms the "why" behind the behavior.

In my helpless, needful hands lies a clue to the motivation behind Ophelia's need to seek her father's guidance in her every decision. I demonstrate me confronting the pulley system and immediately turn myself into Ophelia running to her father to ask about Hamlet's visit to her chamber. Always try to connect your discoveries about behavior in life to characters in drama.

Improvise Marchbanks as he approaches the pulley system. Marchbanks's hands are as unused to mechanical labor as mine, but he is no Ophelia. Look for clues to his responses in the way he deals with the new mechanical marvel, the typewriter, at the beginning of Act II. What is the difference between Marchbanks' responses and the way you and I respond? Why? What do you reveal about Marchbanks when, as him, you approach the pulley system and respond? Try writing a specific description of Marchbanks' responses to the pulley system as though you were in the room watching him.

Dramatic Characters and the Sense of Touch

From the perspective of hands alone, work on these possibilities (let the rest of the body follow effortlessly in response):

•Getting dressed in the morning. What do your hands reveal about you?

•Become Juliet getting dressed. What do your hands do that reveal the Juliet who wants to experience everything that life has to offer?

•What do Juliet's nurse's hands reveal about her?

•Then Arkadina. (I'm a star actress and I can act a beautiful sixteen-year old perfectly.)

•Trigorin, who would rather be whittling a fishing pole than holding a drink at a cocktail party.

•Anya ("In Paris we went up in a balloon!" Doesn't she always have Varya or Dunyasha to help her?)

•Let Varya get dressed and confront the pulley system. Then she goes into the house to prepare it for the day.

Don't figure all these things out beforehand. Take yourself into direct action, and let your senses think about the ideas in their own terms. Let your perceptions think through the possibilities. Don't permit your intellect to make absolute decisions and short-cut the thinking body's modus operandi. Finding out what you don't know about these people will help you articulate future specific tasks for your field-study of humanity.

•Hedda takes the pistol from its case and goes to the window. What does she aim at? A withered leaf clinging to a branch? Judge Brack comes up the walk. Why does she fire the pistol "into thin air"? Judge Brack holds out his hand for the pistol and Hedda makes a decision to hand it over. What does she communicate through this gesture?

•Judge Brack takes out his handkerchief and wipes the pearl knob of his walking stick. With his manicured hands he tips his hat to a lady sitting on her front porch; or, in his study, he pours a brandy and selects a cigar from the wooden box on the desk.

•The sense of touch predominates in the characters of *The Cherry Orchard.* What specific objects most meaningfully help you to create the hands of each of the characters? What are the important objects in each character's life?

•What do you as Gaev, reveal as you touch the bookcase, or reach for candies? Remember, Gaev habitually escapes from the unpleasantness of his present situation into the remembered security of his childhood. He needs Fiers to tie his tie, as much as Anya needs Varya to pin her hair.

• Lubov lets money slip through her fingers, touches her favorite little table, holds her hands out to Anya, tears up her telegram.

• Anya gets Varya to comb out her hair and prepare for bed.

• Gaev sips his coffee, searches for a handkerchief (How successful will he be as a bank teller?) While at the same time:

• Lopakhin wields an axe, looks at his pocket watch, lifts a boulder from the field. Then he takes a book from the bookcase as he waits for Lubov's arrival. He pours a delicate glass of champagne; takes money from his wallet.

• Trofimov, the eternal student, walks with his index finger marking his place in his copy of Karl Marx's writings. His glasses slip to the end of his nose and he fumbles to push them back. His galoshes stick in the mud. How capable will he be of taking productive action when the revolution comes?

• Varya, like a nun, cleans up the house after everyone else has gone to sleep.

• Yasha hurries to pick up the money Lubov drops. Yasha looks to see if he is alone with Dunyasha and then touches her cheek, her shoulder. Yasha drinks champagne in Act IV. What does he reveal about himself by the way he drinks?

Imagine a production of *The Sea Gull* in darkness with only the hands of the characters visible in black light. How does each person reveal character through the sense of touch alone? Note how much you can learn if you disengage your analytical mind and let your "thinking body" explore. Note the opposition between Arkadina's practiced, expressive actress hands and Nina's simple natural grace; between Trigorin, who would rather whittle a fishing pole than get dressed for a book-signing reception and Masha's hands which reach for the snuff box, pull her hair back, play a game of solitaire.

What are Trigorin's and Masha's hands doing at the beginning of Act III? Dr. Dorn's and Polina's in Act I?

SMELL AND TASTE

Smell is the most evocative of the senses. Test yourself with perfume, with the smell of grandmother's house. People's almost subliminal responses to smell evoke immediate, detailed, sensory recollections, not simply vague remembered feelings. There is also growing evidence to suggest that smell (via pheromones) may play a major role in "sexual chemistry."

Do the following:

• Hedda smells the flowers in the house (When was the last time there were so many flowers in her house?). In every room there is the old woman's smell, "like dead flowers after a dance." Do you know that smell? What happens to you in response?

• How acute is Gaev's sense of smell? Lubov's? What clues does the play give you? Be specific.

• Juliet's nurse smells a roast in the kitchen, pours herself a glass of ale, searches for a comfortable chair near the stove. Watch closely. What is her response upon discovering the "dead" Juliet? Whom is she thinking of? Is Juliet most important to her? This clue to her deepest motivated self and to her part in a tragedy about the unbridgeable gulf between adults and young people is here to be discovered.

• Falstaff hefts a mug of beer. Watch how his mouth tastes the alcohol even before he gets it to his lips. Notice his responses as the beer goes down his gullet and hits his stomach.

• Make a toast and drink; now let Hedda toast and drink. Masha of *The Sea Gull* drinks vodka; what do you as Masha reveal about yourself when you lift the glass? When you put it to your lips? What does Masha do as she lets the vodka warm down her throat? What does she reveal by her reactions to the beverage?

Try These:

- Blanche DuBois opens a whiskey bottle and drinks.

- Stanley Kowalski opens a beer and drinks.

- Anna Christie orders a drink.

- Lopakhin buys champagne for the departure from the cherry orchard. How good is the champagne? Let Lopakhin have a drink. Then Yasha.

Compare:

- Hedda drinks. Blanche DuBois drinks. What motivates the need of each woman to drink? How does their behavior reveal these differences? Be specific.

How do eating, drinking and smoking reveal the unspoken? What prompts your friend to light up a cigarette? Even as his voice says that he is untroubled, the way he drags on the cigarette reveals the unspoken. Watch him punctuate a sentence by the way he ducks out the cigarette. Why does Arkadina smoke a cigarette in Act I? Who lights it for her?

The unspoken between people is often revealed as they share food, or by the way they respond to a beverage. How do eating scenes in drama reveal character?

- Trigorin eats lunch and Masha tells the truth as she drinks.

- Solyony and Tusenbach in *Three Sisters* drink as they talk in Act II. What does each reveal about himself and how is their relationship manifested in this shared activity?

- In *Uncle Vanya*, Sonia offers Astrov a bite to eat as she tries to sober him up before he rides off into the dying storm. As they talk, she cuts a piece of cheese, offers it to him, watches him eat, shares with him the circle of light around the sideboard. Even as his words unwittingly hurt her, the two of them share an intimacy that thrills her heart.

- Find other illustrations.

THE KINESTHETIC SENSE

The kinesthetic sense involves the spine and the muscles. When you respond to a flock of birds rising suddenly in a whir from a meadow, or when you stand at the shore and the swell and the rhythm of the waves lifts your spine, the kinesthetic sense sends your muscles and nerves tingling and moving empathically. More than any of the others, the kinesthetic sense seems to "use" the other senses as its partners. When you see a willow tree, your every fibre responds kinesthetically to the graceful sweep of its branches. The sight of people streaming through an airport, accompanied by the boom of distant loudspeakers, causes your muscles to "sense" the vastness of the room; kinesthetically, you become "a person in an airport." Dancing may be defined as letting music stimulate your kinesthetic sense into rhythmic movement. The kinesthetic sense, heightened to an artistically expressive degree, is what Francis Fergusson refers to in the phrase "the histrionic sensibility" in *The Idea of a Theatre* (Princeton University Press, 1949).

What makes you say, "I really like that person," or, "I don't trust him one bit," after only a brief encounter? Your kinesthetic sense is unconsciously perceiving, analyzing and drawing conclusions. From that standpoint, can you describe what is meant by sympathy, empathy, intuition, and instinct? Discover a clear distinction between each of these experiences based on the kinesthetic sense. Illustrate each through improvised behavior. Why does Irina not like "that Solyony of yours," as she says to Tusenbach in Act I?

Animals and children have a direct, clear kinesthetic response to life. Their muscles interpret for them. How does a stray dog "know" that an approaching human being is a friend or a threat? It will respond positively to someone whose spine and voice are inviting, even though their words may be threatening. A child, in response to fireworks or the lighting of a Christmas tree, uses a fully-freed kinesthetic sense. It is unnerving to observe a child who has lost, or never had, a responsive kinesthetic sense; we talk about how "grown-up" such a child is. But we delight in an old person and say how "young" they are when they are still kinesthetically responsive.

Note your own kinesthetic responses to people and your environment. Observe how others respond to the same stimuli. Study a truly kinesthetically responsive person to help heighten your own kinesthetic sense.

Actors need a highly-developed, deeply-responsive kinesthetic sense. Do some free-form dancing to free your kinesthetic self: use sweeping romantic music, then rock, jazz, African, South American. Go into your room, put colored lightbulbs in, take off all your clothes (if that will free you). Play the music loud and simply let your body go; let it respond, let your muscles and your kinesthetic sensibilities respond fully and freely to each kind of music. Improvise extreme melodramatic stories to the sweeping passages of Tchaikovsky. Follow the example of the animated soundtrack from Walt Disney's *Fantasia* and respond to Beethoven or Bartok. Enact the entire *Sorcerer's Apprentice* to the music. Improvise "The Masha Dream Ballet" for a nonsense production of *The Sea Gull*. Try "Juliet's Nurse Dances Her Fondest Wishes" or the "Hedda Frees Herself in Her Dreams" solo. Invent other examples.

Do extreme, expansive actions: Jump and shout, stretch out your arms, stick out your tongue, roll your eyes and flex your fingers as you sing a nonsense melody. Scrunch yourself up into a tiny ball; make fists, squint your eyes and whimper like a little animal in a trap. Do a wild, free-form version of the Monty Python "Ministry of Silly Walks." Float on the air and ripple like a chiffon scarf in the wind. Do an exaggerated version of being struck by lightning. Sustain it for several minutes. Fence with freedom, leap onto stone walls and run and jump with joy. Play an exaggerated game of hopscotch. Find out which of these activities embarrasses or inhibits you. Work to free yourself from your inhibition as you make up your own exercises. Do anything to free the kinesthetic sense.

Watching documentaries of Walt Disney's animators is especially illuminating. Down on all fours, they study a deer to get the "feel" of its movements into their muscles. They then translate that understanding into pen and ink and Bambi. They watch their faces in mirrors, or study the slow-motion movements of a fat vaudevillian dancer for Doc in *Snow White and the Seven Dwarfs*. They let their muscles get the feel of mud bubbling in a cauldron before sketching the volcanoes in "The Rite of Spring" section from *Fantasia*.

Develop a kinesthetic sense that is a natural response to every kind of rhythm. Choose a favorite selection of classical music. Kinesthetically conduct a classroom of students or an imaginary symphony orchestra. Note the kinesthetic differences between Mozart and Satie, Shostakovich and Brahms. Let yourself respond in movement terms to each kind of music. What conclusions do you draw? In an interview with David Frost, Isaac Stern demonstrated the various kinds of vibrato appropriate for different composers of the violin. Are there implications for approaches to the kinesthetic music underlying Shakespeare, Moliere and Chekhov? Imagine the symphonic Ibsen and conduct it; an overture to *Arms and the Man*; Macbeth's theme music; the Masha and Vershinin love theme. Invent your own illustrations and conduct them, dance to them, sing them.

Spine and the Kinesthetic Sense: Youth and Age

Concentrate on the big muscles of the lower back. Observe in young people how they are responsive, flexible, alive. Skateboarding, rollerblading, running along the beach, jumping out of a chair, leaping across stones in a brook, stepping onto a platform, dancing of any kind: all of these absolutely depend on these muscles. Try it and see.

Then, observe the spine of the old woman ahead on the sidewalk as young people come near her. Watch the muscles of her lower back tense to hold on as the young spines spin and pivot and rush headlong beyond her. Watch an old person try to step up onto a high curb or get into a bus. Let your own body discover the "why" behind the behavior you observe. Watch for adjustments being made to keep the gravity centered; the body is never off balance for very long as an old person takes tiny steps, and shifts weight quickly from side to side, and barely lifts the feet off the ground.

Observe the middle-aged spine on its way to becoming inflexible. It tries to be young and expressive, fighting gravity's increasing effects on the muscles of the lower back while dancing, or engaging in athletic activities. (What implications for Judge Brack's spine and kinesthetic sense do you find in Ibsen's description of him as "a man of forty-five, thickset, yet well-built, with supple movements,...a walking suit a bit too youthful for his age...."?)

Balance is very much rooted in these muscles of the lower back. A baby taking its first faltering steps as it discovers the components of balance is an elemental illustration of the kinesthetic sense in action, of developing nonconscious awareness. Become the little child who does not understand walking and observe the part played by the muscles of the lower back and abdomen.

Try these exercises:

• Assume an interesting standing position with only one foot on the floor. Reach your arms in opposing directions. Let one direction pull your body slowly out of equilibrium. Follow the force until you pull yourself completely off balance. At the last moment, just before you would fall, bring the other foot down and immediately lift the previously anchored foot. Let yourself regain balance slowly, naturally. Arrest a moment. Enjoy the sensation of balance happening. Then let another force pull your arms in opposing directions and you are off again. Repeat the process until your whole body loves the interplay of resistance of forces that is balance.

• Walk an imaginary tight rope. Sense the joy involved in a flexible, kinesthetic body as it explores the dynamic interplay of forces creating balance.

When a student fell from a third story window recently and was paralyzed, part of the horror on campus was rooted in the belief that young people shouldn't lose their balance and should always bounce back unharmed if they do. Such whispers of the mortality of youth always elicit gasps of shock.

Young people have a terrific sense of balance, which they can recover almost effortlessly. At sixty years of age, the School's administrative assistant insists that she can balance on one leg to pull on a boot. Why? Balance means resilience, and she is determined to maintain a youthful flexibility for as long as she can.

Romeo and Juliet and *The Sea Gull* both dramatize, in part, the perennial conflicts between youth and age. What external stimuli cause your youthful spine to lift with joy, to stand on tip-toe and open your eyes wide with excitement? Find the stimuli that will touch off in you the eager, life-motivated spine of Juliet. Run freely along the marble halls of an old library and out onto the lawn; in the garden find a flower you have never seen before. Let a lake or a field or a parking lot become the seaport of Verona. A ship with billowing white sails arrives bearing treasures from the East! Run up to the balcony and to catch a glimpse of the ship on the horizon. Turn yourself into Juliet through simple, motivated responses to concrete stimuli.

Find a Romeo spine, eager to run toward life, to ward off an attack from a hidden enemy in the side alley, to leap to the top of the wall to pick a ripe apple from an overhanging limb. Find an equally vital Benvolio who is always ready to render assistance to his friends. (Why do Lord and Lady Montague choose Benvolio to answer their questions about Romeo?) Find the poet-entertainer spine of Mercutio. (Note Mercutio's capacity for pain that is in the Treplev spine, the Marchbanks spine. How and why does Mercutio deal with it? With what results?)

Consider the adults. Where in the contemporary world will you find the Nurse? Where will you look for the burdened old spine that moans and groans? How and why is she motivated? Her nose smells a roast beef cooking, her lips smack in anticipation of the juices; her creature comforts have become more important to her than Juliet's well-being. What can turn you into the Nurse who wants nothing more than a shady spot and a cold beer? The Nurse may be delightful, but she is blind to Juliet's deepest needs. Our laughter at her stems from our recognition of a complaining grand-mother, or a housekeeper whose conversation is all work but whose greatest pleasure is taking a load off her feet when no one is looking.

Friar Laurence has the spine of a likable well-meaning adult who hands out simple solutions to complex human problems. Contrast Romeo's young spine as it bounds on sprightly feet into the Friar's herb garden, eagerly seeking his blessing, with the Friar's set-tled spine and steady padding feet. Begin to sense the opposition of forces in a drama that drives two vivacious young people to the trag-ic point of choosing death over life.

• In *The Sea Gull*, Arkadina's determination to maintain youth-fulness is in direct contrast to the healthy natural youth of Nina: find the clues at the beginning of Act II. Why does Arkadina take her frustration out on Masha? Can you sense the drama inherent in the opposition of their spines?

• What are the implications for Treplev's youthful spine even in Act I? What has happened by Act IV?

• Chronologically, Medvedenko is a youth, but, experientially, what has happened to his young spine?

• Masha expresses her clinical depression by deadening all kinesthetic responsiveness. She seeks to paralyze the longings of her heart with drink.

• What has happened to Nina's soaring sea gull spine of Act I by the time she enters in Act IV? Sketch the two spines, then bring them to life with kinesthetic spine and muscle comprehension.

• Arkadina's spine compared to Nina's and Treplev's doesn't change. What implications can we draw for the meanings communicated in the play? Create the progress of each character's spine.

Always ask the question: "What is motivation?" Ask how it expresses itself in terms of the actor's response and perception to reveal the mystery of human behavior.

SENSORY DEPRIVATION

You can tell which of your roommates is coming down the hall simply by hearing footsteps. Put a blindfold on or turn out the lights. A classmate enters the room: what can you tell about him simply from listening to his footsteps? Listen for rhythm, balance, weight placement, speed, relationship to gravity, length of stride. Let yourself become him, and recreate the same aural impressions. Discover what accounts for all that you heard. Work to let your body naturally and easefully come to comprehension. Others should join in and demonstrate different qualities as the class finds another sensory response avenue toward understanding human behavior.

Friar Laurence says this about Juliet's footsteps as she enters the church to be married:

Here comes the body. O, so light a foot

Will ne'er wear out the everlasting flint;

A lover may bestride the gossamers

That idles in the wanton summer air,

And yet not fall; so light is vanity.

· *(II, vi 16-20)*

Can you create that step as part of your Juliet? Is it true of her only as she hastens to her wedding?

• Create the Nina whom a deaf person sees coming along the path to Treplev's house.

• Create the Nurse whom a blind person hears coming into the garden after her day seeking out Romeo.

•Devise other illustrations from the plays we focus on in this book.

Blindfold yourself and study singly several interesting objects. Avoid simple identification. Rather, the goal is to respond, to explore with your senses, to let associations play through. At Theatre Arts U, Kyle was handed a wet tea bag. He smiled instantly and began to handle it surely but gingerly. There was a glow to his face and an unaccustomed warmth to his voice. "I live on a farm," he said. "I have helped deliver puppies and calves." The rest of the class observes, perceives, comes to discoveries about Kyle and about the revelatory nature of sensory response. As always, they recreate their discoveries later in terms of their own behavior.

•Become Nina and explore one of the objects.

•Let Romeo do this exercise.

What do you discover about character through the senses? Then those who observe get a chance to demonstrate what they discovered.

ALL SENSES

Marchbanks, Osvald, Mercutio, Treplev all share the poet's sensibility: all senses respond to the world intensely, sometimes painfully, to even the most joyful of experiences. Do you know someone with the poet's sensibility?

Take the characters in *Romeo and Juliet, The Sea Gull, The Cherry Orchard, Candida, Hedda Gabler*. Create a characterization from spine alone, hands alone, eyes alone. For example, *Hedda Gabler*:

• Spine: Hedda's trapped Victorian woman's spine.

• Hands: Hedda's refined lady's hands are willing and able to handle a pistol like a man, shoot it right on target, ride a horse.

• Eyes: Responsive eyes see life and face it directly; then, they conceal their response. Why? What is important to Hedda? What does she fear? Where are you likely to find these eyes? Why does no one in the play recognize the eyes of a trapped woman? Hedda looks at the living room. What specifically does she see? The ugly flower-patterned carpet, the table with the filigree-framed picture, the heavy green velvet draperies. Her response?

•Ears: Hedda hears Tesman padding about upstairs. She hears the educated, witty tones of Judge Brack's voice.

•Muscles (Kinesthetic): Hedda's muscles respond as Aunt Julia comes toward her to kiss her.

Where will you find the eyes of a Judge Brack, a man at the top of a man's world? His eyes see the curves of a woman's breasts, the line of her dress, the foot tapping with boredom as she talks and he adds them up to: A Bored Woman. A smile crosses his lips.

Look for the erect, open spine of the confident man in a man's world. Listen for the smooth, oily voice and the wide charming smile that melts other people's reserve. Look for the careful, deliberate, relaxed walk and the manicured hands that touch so delicately, that love to hold fine crystal wine glasses, that choose the perfect cravat. Ibsen gives him a monocle. Why? Begin by taking him for his afternoon stroll down the street, walking stick in hand. He sees a woman sitting on a swing on the front porch, her foot tapping away. He smiles and tips his hat. She waves and her husband comes to the gate to greet him. On he goes, hat gleaming in the sun, freshly polished shoes tapping, his ring catching the light as he lifts his cane to the woman picking roses in the next yard. Improvise until the well-known, well-liked, confident, genial, man-about-town Judge Brack spine is created, until you respond clearly and naturally with that spine motivated to be the cock-of-the-walk in this man's world.

Read the last scene of Thornton Wilder's *Our Town* as Emily says good-bye to life. Become your own Emily. Surprise yourself by discovering the sensory experiences you would most poignantly say good-bye to. Without thinking, simply let yourself say good-bye to a favorite visual sensation, to a sound you love, to a touch stimulus that you enjoy, to the kinesthetic experience you would miss the most. Discover how important your senses really are to your humanity. At the most fundamental level, human beings are motivated to live. Find out what "to live" really, elementally, means.

Then try this last example using characters from plays:

• Let yourself be Candida and say good-bye to your favorite sensory stimuli.

• Lubov actually does this in the play, doesn't she? Create the moment specifically.

• Try it with the Juliet who starts the play.

• Juliet's Nurse.

• Add your own examples.

2

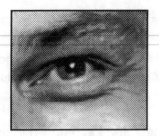

The
Senses
at Work

I love to sit and watch people.
I love to sit and listen to people....the most useful and indeed
fascinating tool of [the actor's] work.

— Daniel Day-Lewis

Response

To be alive in your world is to be responsive to its stimuli. For example, when you go to the harbor you can truly see the color of the lake or the pattern of boat masts at dock. Your sense of sight stimulates a response in you; perhaps you smile, take in a deep breath of bracing air, make a mental photograph. You hear the waves lapping against the rocks, the metallic clicking of ropes against masts in the breeze, and your senses respond. But what does it mean to respond?

Observe yourself and others in response to the stimuli around you. What do your eyes automatically see as significant?. What subtle response does your body have to the smell, the sounds, the "feel" of a harbor? What do you do that reveals the open-air space of the harbor? What changes occur that reveal time of day, or year, or weather? Be specific.

Go to the harbor with someone else. Note your responses to each other and the harbor both as individuals and as a couple. How does the relationship between you influence your responses to the harbor? Be as specific and as literal as possible when you answer such questions. You are exploring the reality of "human response" so that you may apply it to the art of acting.

Note the many levels of response as the two of you are walking along the dock, talking about theatre. Your eyes watch a sailboat; your ears hear the lapping of water at the dock; your nose catches the smell of fish; your fingers play absently with the napkin around an ice cream cone as you discuss the state of American theatre, or British versus American acting. Much of this multi-layered series of responses is nonconscious, but your total sensual being is always completely aware of these specific stimuli.

As you talk, a little boy fishing at the dock lifts his pole and screams in delight at the fish twisting on the end. You and your partner see this; perhaps you share the event (How? Be specific.), even letting it find its way into words. Unless the event assumes real significance (perhaps the boy slips into the harbor), you return to your conversation and your senses carry on.

As I sit in my apartment writing this chapter, my motivated spine is alive in its basic drive to teach; my immediate objective is to communicate the nature of sensory response. Suddenly, my concentration is shattered by a loud, harsh, male voice. I catch my breath and my spine stiffens in anticipation: the people upstairs are having another argument. A shrill counter-attack from a whining female voice makes my eyes flinch against the violence, and before I finished writing that sentence, hard stomping footsteps shook the ceiling of my room. My whole body has snapped to attention in anticipation of any sound of dangerous violence, which will send me scurrying into action (Should I call the police, or leave my apartment, or turn up my stereo to drown out the noise?). Associations of terrible family arguments in my childhood have activated additional responses which transcend my teacher-writer response.

As I was writing that last sentence, the radiator in the bathroom began to hiss and I responded. My mind and body continue to concentrate on the immediate objective of writing while my deeper associations, activated by the sensory stimuli in the apartment above me, play through me with increasing insistence. I am free to respond to many peripheral stimuli and continue to write, but some part of me is still arrested, anticipating the resumption of the terrible argument. Human response to stimuli is a complex tapestry of phenomena interwoven at many levels.

The thinking body responds simultaneously in various degrees of consciousness or awareness with the human mind. The many threads and strands of response work concurrently to create a total sense of self in any one moment, at any one time. One degree of awareness is stimulated by the thought responses to specific details of environment: at the harbor, even as you speak, you see the ice cream drip onto your shirt, you take the paper napkin to wipe, you hear the band playing somewhere in the park. Another set of stimuli leads to vocal response: the topic of discussion (American theatre), or significant stimuli ("Oh look! That boy just fell into the water."). An arresting stimulus strikes a "lower-level," non-conscious note in your being ("My ice cream is dripping"), part of which is verbal (intonation, stress, range, pitch, rate, pause, silence, length of thought, interruption), most of which is not. On a deeper level are the currents that carry you through your life. (Fears about your ability to act drove you outdoors to the security found in the sights and sounds of the harbor), and the immediate currents carrying you through the present situation (Your friend gives you moral support. Expressed how?).

Most of these "levels of response" remain unexpressed verbally yet they are constantly active. At any given moment, they comprise the forceful threads of your preoccupations, directly or indirectly accounting for the actual words you choose and the vocal characteristics of your speech. Non-conscious responses will occasionally find their way into conscious thought, but they are generally expressed in non-conscious areas of behavior, such as the tapping of a foot, or the stiffening of a spine; the hand that clenches, or the fingers that nervously pluck at the napkin, even as the conversation continues on another topic. On a more inward level, mental activities include silent words, (Doesn't a part of your mind think in words?), and images (Doesn't a part of your mind, or most of it, "think" in images?), which form and dissolve in the multiplicity of associations that you bring to your sensory responses. Simultaneously, your thinking body responds and discovers, coming to conclusions in its own terms.

A good actor must become a person alive to the world, evaluating and discovering the mystery of human response; whose "thinking body" stores up such awarenesses with deep understanding; and whose totality responds artfully, on cue, to the many levels of stimuli creating any dramatic situation.

Study the process of sensory response by observing yourself and others in response to a variety of stimuli. Take note of how each one appeals to each of your senses. Observe how each preoccupying thread promotes a response in what your eyes and hands do; note the flow of your thoughts as you speak; feel the rhythms of your walk; discover which associations elicit verbal or nonverbal responses. Note the influence of your relationship with whoever accompanies you. Begin with these examples:

Places

- a walk in the country
- a day at the amusement park
- visit to your old hometown
- a shopping trip to the mall

Situations

- an argument, indoors or outdoors   (Try each of these: Indoors at a restaurant or in your bedroom; outdoors at an ice-skating rink or a city street corner.)

- a date (with someone you know well, with someone you really want to impress, with someone you dislike)

- a farewell party for friends who are moving

- a visit from your spouse's childhood friend

Consider the various stimuli that influence responses, which reveal character, and relationships, in situations. Remember that "thinking about" isn't enough: follow through on these ideas, because an actor is primarily a student of human behavior. Do the work. Learn to make active illustrative learning of all aspects of living.

I urge your observant and perceptive actor-self to study actual, real-life situations. Be alert to what people really do, and become a student of genuine human behavior. Too much of contemporary acting is rooted in what young actors watch and imitate in other actors. The goal of your acting is the illumination of the mystery of human life, so your learning must be rooted in its study.

The more actual reality you perceive and store up, the more of it you can bring to your exploration through improvisation. It is more important to enact real behavior in true situations than to squander improvisational time on contrived examples in which you become a truck driver who hates to tip and your acting partner becomes a waitperson who needs extra money. To be of any value, improvisational work must be based on reality; otherwise, it becomes an exercise in how clever the individual actors can be. Your goal is to perceive life from the playwright's point of view and to truthfully create that life on the stage. To cast that creation in meaningful form for an audience, you must root your creativity in the fundamental truths of human behavior.

An actor's artistry is to discover, create and communicate to an audience the meaning of human behavior as it is organized and patterned by a playwright.

Let's take the example of going to the harbor and apply it to *The Sea Gull* as Dorn and Polina walk from Sorin's house to Kostya's outdoor stage. Dorn is a doctor who enjoys the comfort of life: his lower spine settles comfortably into his pelvis, his walk is deliberate and confident, with a smooth, regular rhythm. (Why? Have you observed such a person?) His ribcage lifts, open to the stimuli of the world; his head sits high on his neck; his eyes see past the lake to the European capitals he has visited. Unengaged by company, sated like a person who leaves the table after a rich meal, he whistles absently into the gathering dusk. (What is important to him?)

Take Dorn out onto the porch for an after-dinner cigar or, perhaps, as an intermission from Arkadina's entertaining stories. The sun has just gone down; the air is close with a gathering storm; the crickets have begun singing. Perhaps everyone is gathered to hear Trigorin play the piano as Arkadina sings a favorite *entr-acte*. Sorin comes in and asks everyone to go out to the little theatre since the play must start at the moment the moon comes up over the lake. With a charming exit line, Dorn takes his leave and Polina follows.

By what inevitable series of determining experiences has Polina come to this moment in her life? Improvise and discover.

Arkadina, of course, decides to sing one more song.

With a friend, take the Dorn and Polina walk from the house to Treplev's stage. Pay no attention to what you will say; simply discover your responses to each other and to the sensory stimuli of the walk. Afterward, write out a description of what you discover about each of the people. What does Polina want so desperately to say to Dorn? Why does she not do what she wants? What significant stimuli does Chekhov suggest? What do you discover about the nature of response?

Anyone who has truly perceived the birthday celebration of the youngest child in a loving family will know how to strike the most positive note for the party in Act I of *Three Sisters*. Create in detail the name-day interactions that initiate the forceful opening of the play: "Father died a year ago today, the fifth of May, your name day, Irina." (Why is this not a wistful minor key?) These people are not the morbid, maudlin characters that Chekhov is traditionally accused of creating; nor are they the silly, incomprehensible cartoons that recent productions have given us in the name of so-called "Chekhovian comedy." They are people just like us.

Devise your own learning system. Set daily tasks:

1. "Today I will observe the unspoken responses at play in an human interaction":
   * in the emergency room of the local hospital.
   * at a diner frequented by regular customers.
   * in a nursing home.

Study, observe, store up with comprehension.

2. "Today I will concentrate on the responses of someone who is engaged in a passionate conversation":
- a friend talking about her relationship with her parents.
- an intense interaction in a restaurant, or at the student union, or on the street.

Focus on the actual process of response that creates any human interaction.

3. "Today I will study myself objectively even as I am fully engaged in a charged situation."
Go on with more illustrations.

Atmosphere and Mood

A group of people meet on the beach in the bright afternoon sun. They swim, drink, smoke, sunbathe. Some play Frisbee while another goes for a pizza. The sun moves across the sky; some leave and others arrive. The group moves to a nearby picnic table as the shadows lengthen and the air changes. Across the park a boom box plays and conversations develop. Two people lean against a tree trunk. Somebody pulls at the grass around the tree as he talks. Another sits silently looking at the lake where the colorful sailboats linger in the last light of a late summer day.

Every place and situation has its own "feel." What accounts for such a mood? What human sensory responses to what specific stimuli create what we call "atmosphere"? (Michael Chekhov assumed that a place has an atmosphere even when no human beings are present to respond to it.) Develop your awareness of the elements that create the mood and tempo of a specific environment: a bank, the lobby of a clinic, a church on a wedding day, a playground. Take note of what stimuli all your senses respond to. What are the resulting physical, muscular and sensory responses? Observe individual contributions to the aggregate creation of an atmosphere. Re-create the stimuli and the responses and come to an active discovery of mood, rhythm and tempo as they apply to environment.

• Go to the lake on a calm day. Let yourself respond. In your room, recreate the experience through your sensory and muscle responses. Then go back on a roily, windy evening. Back in your room, repeat the exercise.

• Go to the town public gardens.

• Go to the town library in the early morning, at dinner time, at closing time.

• Find a church, a temple, or a mosque. Let the environmental factors play upon you until you are responding in simpatico with the place. Account for differences.

• Study the interactions of people at an all-night diner at three in the morning on a Saturday. How does time of night become translated into individual and group behavior? What specifically contributes to the atmosphere and the tempo of the place? What particular factors encourage the interplay among patrons who frequent this kind of restaurant? A "mood piece," such as Lanford Wilson's *Balm in Gilead*, depends upon actors sucessfully creating such fluctuations in atmosphere.

• Go to a fine restaurant and note the totally different rhythm and feel from the twenty-four-hour diner. Account for the disparity in observed and perceived specific human behavioral responses. Try a vegetarian cafe, a Chinese carry-out, an Italian family restaurant, a sushi bar.

• How and why does the tempo of the medical clinic differ from that of the bank? Be specific with your answers by using direct experience. Avoid relying on general impressions and stereotyped ideas.

Try these:

• a grocery store at morning rush hour

• the same store late in the evening

• an Italian-Catholic funeral

• a Jewish or Polish wedding

• an outdoor farmer's market

• an inner-city grade school

Ask your "thinking body" what causes the beat, and whether there are opposing rhythmic lines. What is the undercurrent, and how is it manifested? Note the musical qualities of assonance, dissonance and counterpoint. Account for the similarities and the differences and recreate them in terms of stimuli and response.

What accounts for the characteristic rhythm of your own home? How and why does it differ from your friend's house? Be specific. How would you answer these questions if you visited Hedda's house? The Gaev estate? Candida's and Morell's home? Elsinore? Inverness? Improvise. Write a letter home about each of these describing, in detail, which specific elements directly influence human responses to create tempo.

Part of Chekhov's greatness lies in his ability to incorporate the effects of weather, seasons, and time of day into the dynamic fabric of his plays. Place and environment serve to focus the drama in the individual responses of his characters.

The atmosphere of Act I of *The Sea Gull* is the houseparty that is the social high point of Arkadina's annual summer vacation in the country. Years ago, when there were six thriving estates around the lake, these parties lasted for days and had scores of guests, music, laughter, and sexual intrigue. Recently the parties have dwindled; Arkadina's only guests are her ailing old brother Leonid; her son Treplev; Shamraev, the steward of the estate, and his wife Polina; their daughter Masha, and her suitor, the teacher Medvedenko. A pleasant holdover from earlier times is Arkadina's old friend and former lover, Dr. Yevgeny Dorn, who still brings his sophisticated wit and cosmopolitan charm to the gathering.

Translate through improvisation the following details in terms of specific stimuli and individual sensory responses: The day has been lazy, perhaps with croquet on the lawn, or a picnic. The night will be warm, but far off a storm threatens. There will be drinking and dining. Arkadina, with only Polina and Masha as her competition, is the enchanting center of attention, entertaining everyone with stories of the theatre season past. The barking dogs have already begun to disturb her sleep, but she has not yet grown as bored and irritable as she will be by Act II. Today, spirits are high and she can bask in the admiration of family and friends.

Add these elements: Arkadina has brought her young lover of less than a year, Boris Alexeyevitch Trigorin. This is his first visit and she will be watchful. Treplev has worked on a play that she views as a deliberate affront to her artistry. Nina, Treplev's childhood friend, has developed into an enchanting, lovely young woman. At moonrise, when everyone should gather round the piano before supper to sing *entr-actes* from Arkadina's plays, they will all have to trek out to the lake to see Nina starring in Treplev's annoying playlet. On the surface, Arkadina enchants with a bright voice and a gay manner, but beneath she grows furious. Such is the atmosphere from which the specific action of Act I emerges.

Do the same for Act III. Arkadina is finally going to get out of this boring summer place and back to the theatre and being the center of the excitement of Moscow. Bags have to be packed, horses harnessed, carriages brought around, baskets of food to be prepared, last-minute lists to be checked. The atmosphere is kinetic, exciting, the preparation for departure. Playing against this, of course, are individual character motivations, needs, responses: Treplev has kept to the shadows since his suicide attempt; Masha is drinking more heavily than usual (She tries to stay out of Treplev's way and away from her mother in the kitchen); Trigorin hasn't much to pack and has retired to the lunch room for a little quiet time and some last-minute note-taking on Masha, who has been a subject of his for weeks; Sorin takes advantage of the situation to plan a trip to town. These are individual actions that create the play's rhythms and counter-rhythms, the atmosphere and the activity which absolutely engage the entire household.

The atmosphere, tempo, and rhythms of *The Cherry Orchard*, Act II are not confined to that part of the estate presented on the stage. Think beyond the confines of the stage to the whole estate. What has been happening today at the house? How far from the main house is the little shrine and the bench where Act II actually takes place? Why is this place special? How do the servants find their way here?

As for the group coming back from lunch in town, whose idea was it to leave the carriage and walk back to the house? Why? Why not stop at another place on the estate?

Improvise to explore these questions. Avoid answering purely intellectually and acting accordingly. Rather, organize your thinking about the total environment, the atmosphere, and interactive tempos of this part of the play. Create the entire Gaev estate, not just the part that appears on stage. Find a place in a nearby park to improvise. Turn the little ice cream stand into a ruined chapel, the trees into the orchard. Create the atmosphere of Act II through sensory and kinesthetic responses. Note the significant elements: sunset, a toppled shrine, a mourning dove in the distance, a river rushing softly by behind you. Come back to the classroom and recreate it all in meaningful detail.

Create the mood, the rhythms, the tempo, the atmosphere, of:

- Opening scene(s) of *Romeo and Juliet*
- The varying moods of each act of *Candida*
- The morning of Act I of *Hedda Gabler*
- The last act of *Hedda*
- Elsinore at the beginning of *Hamlet*

Response is a complex phenomenon, difficult to isolate and study. In order for it to be happening truthfully, it must be non-conscious. But as an actor, you must consciously develop an unconscious underpinning of your art just as athletes concentrate on the individual response processes that make up their sport: basketball players must consciously study the intricacies of dribbling, passing and shooting so that, during the game, they can simply let these things happen and concentrate on the actual playing.

Be constantly on the lookout for the revelatory behavior of yourself and others as a part of your daily life. Eventually, such study will become second-nature, just as a photographer always sees composition and a painter sees light and color.

Response Precedes Emotion

When describing a powerful interaction, a person may say, "Boy, was I angry," or, "I have never been so embarrassed in my life," or, "I was hurt and I didn't know what to do." Such statements do not describe what actually happened; they offer generalized emotional descriptions of the experience. In fact, the person was not just angry, embarrassed or hurt: These words simply describe, after the fact, a state of being that comprised an infinite number of stimuli-response experiences. In an attempt to recreate such an experience, actors often make the mistake of taking that generalized patina of an emotional state and acting through it. They focus only on the stimuli that relate directly to the emotional state; they respond only to the words, investing their sensory attention in the other person, who becomes the focus of their responses. We have all witnessed actors who create "sad" characters by using a teary weepy voice that no actual human being has ever used. When we recreate highly-charged experiences, we forget the myriad levels of response that created the situation as well as what place the vocal aspects actually occupied in the total experience.

"Response" doesn't mean emotion or attitude. Emotion may be viewed as an after-effect of response, but it is rarely the stimulus. "Attitude" is usually a manufactured substitute for a truly motivated spine. In both cases, this leads to fakery in acting, however emotionally compelling it may seem.

Recently, at Theatre Arts U., Tom was working on Hamlet's first soliloquy. He was alternately angry and sad, despondent and fitful, sustaining each emotion for however many lines seemed appropriate. As an audience member, however, all I saw was how angry Hamlet was, or how sad or despondent. I wasn't really hearing what he was saying, nor was I experiencing what was happening to him because he was not truly responding to specific stimuli. He did not communicate any immediate need to express those specific ideas. Any words would have done because he was experiencing only the general emotions of sadness, anger, and disappointment, for which there really is no need for words. I certainly got no suspenseful kinesthetic sense of impending action. In other words, there was no drama.

"Tell me one thing Hamlet wants to do right now," I said.

After a moment: "He wants to run after Claudius and spin him around and punch him."

"All right, get ready to do that." He did. "Good. Now, what else might he do?"

"He could fall on the floor and start crying."

"Then do that," and as he began to, "but keep in your muscles the impulse to run after Claudius." He did.

"He could throw himself onto the throne and hang onto the memory of his father sitting there."

"Do that, but keep the need to punch out Claudius (Be ready to do it as soon as I clap my hands) and keep active the capacity to collapse onto the floor in tears. (Be ready and able to do it the moment I yell, 'Collapse!')" He was becoming more and more animated, ready, capable of action.

"He could run up to his room and slam the door and never come out again."

"Add it."

"He could call out to his mother and then throw himself at her feet and hold onto her and beg her not to go to bed with Claudius."

"Do it."

By embodying each action, Tom began to discover what Hamlet wants to do, why he wants to do it, and why he does not do it. He achieved all this in terms of positively-motivated behavior rather than general negative emotion. We began to discover how Hamlet's words are activated by the struggle between taking action and exercising restrain, finally expressing the essential experience that has shattered his world: "married with mine uncle." Now we have drama where before we had only emotion.

• Apply this approach to the Arkadina/Treplev "bandage scene." What really happens in such an argument? It's hard to be objective because we get so subjectively involved we only remember "how we felt." We must concentrate on what actually happened, what interactive responses actually took place, what conflicts of interest were at war within each and between both persons.

• Apply the idea to Nina and Treplev in Act IV. So often, Nina is portrayed as a neurotic on the verge of a nervous breakdown, and Treplev as a spineless wimp. What must really be happening if Treplev can finally say, "You have found your way," and let Nina leave? Find a metaphoric or real-life situation that will help actors truly understand what is actually happening. Have you ever watched someone come out of a troubling fever? How might that experience apply to this situation? Literalize the metaphor of Nina's dilemma.

• Apply to Hedda's final scene with Brack. Why is the usual choice often passionless and conversational or simplistic, overemotional melodrama?

• Apply to the Mrs. Alving's and Pastor Manders' "guilty mother" scene.

Why are "memory speeches" so often delivered in a trance-like way, practically halting the forward progress of the entire play, just so that one character can sink into a hazy, emotion-laden reminiscence? Find out instead what the character responds to in the present that necessitates the story. What series of moment-by-moment responses, negotiations, adjustments with the other characters in the situation cause the story to be told the way it is? In other words, how is the story forwarding the drama on stage in the present?

• What is happening in the present that touches off Treplev's "memory speech" to Sorin while they await everyone's arrival for the play?

• What positive realization prompts Olga to speak at the beginning of *Three Sisters?*

• In *Streetcar Named Desire* what inspires Blanche Dubois' story to Mitch about the death of her young husband?

Responses to People

Let us focus our attention on specific responses to other people in any situation. Besides words, to what else do you respond? What are your kinesthetic muscles responding to? What's happening to your breathing, as you listen? Why? What are your eyes and your spine non-consciously responding to as your hands do something completely opposite? Notice how, besides your voice and your emotions, you respond with other parts of your totality.

As a person speaks to you, note your responses to eyes, to muscle shifts, note what happens when the other person's spine tenses and the eyes drop. Note your response to hands, to tension in the other's muscles, to head movements. Besides the actual words, note how tone, volume, changes in range, pitch, and rhythm affect you. Note your response to the unspoken, the concealed, the implied. How are these communicated? These responses are almost always non-conscious, but an actor's art is to make a conscious study of the complex processes of daily human response.

Response may be subtle, but it is always physical and it always precedes emotion; it is the reason for the emotion to which your intellect later gives a descriptive word. Emotion is the result of your responses, not their fuel nor the reason for their existence.

You may say, "But when I'm angry, it's because I'm angry that I say this or that." As an actor, focus on the conflict between opposing needs to do something which results in the complex series of responses that we label with single emotion words: anger, fear, joy, etc. It is in the highly-charged conflict that drama is located, not in the chemical after-effects that we call emotion.

Listen to the responsive body so that you may learn to hear the unspoken. Let actions speak to you louder than words. If someone says, "I really think you're talented," what do you hear and respond to besides the words? Do you perceive truth in his eyes? Do his eyes look away, or narrow, or conceal? Do they confirm? What does the spine, rather than the voice, say? What story do the hands tell, or the tone and volume of the voice? Note that you respond to all of these, not just the words, "I really think you're talented," even if the next thing the speaker says to you is, "So why are you so boring?"

As dialogue in a play, your next line will probably be directly inspired by the last words spoken to you, but your responding being was not necessarily preparing itself for your next line; it was responding instant-by-instant, stimulus-by-stimulus, idea-by-idea, perhaps anticipating some quite different response, just as the "boring" statement came out and derailed you.

Study this phenomenon in life and invent improvisations to illustrate your observations. Make a habit of responding on several levels at once, even in anticipation of the expected response of the other.

What does Treplev expect Nina to do when he lays the seagull at her feet? What exactly does his body prepare itself to respond to? What, in fact, does Nina actually do? With what response in Treplev?

Subtext

It has no doubt occurred to you by now that, at any given moment, people are fully conscious of the minutest part of the total stimuli playing upon them and the multitude of responses their total beings are making. These multi-varied non-verbal layers of response are what constitute "subtext." Subtext is too often thought of as the emotional underpinning to, (What is he actually feeling?) or the ulterior motive for (What is she really thinking?) the words. Actors occasionally force such false elements into their acting as they "search for the subtext." This misreading was taken to an absurd extreme recently when a friend questioned a colleague's casting of a thin actress to play Olga in *Three Sisters*. "But Olga must be fat," he said, "because at the beginning of the play she says, 'I've grown so thin.'" I felt as though I had suddenly been thrust into one of Lewis Carroll's wicked little parodies.

Study subtext in action around you. In any situation, what sensory stimuli are at play? Which do you respond to most con-sciously? Why? Can you identify other individual responses to these situational stimuli? Which are significant, direct determiners of group response? Which stimuli/response processes do not find their way into words? Why? When do undercurrents of response suddenly burst into words? An obvious example is the annoying rep-etition of a sound that finally causes someone to shout, "Will you stop that!" Find more meaningful, revelatory illustrations.

Apply to Drama

Carry into plays these ideas about the nature of the respons-es that exist beneath, beyond, outside of, the words people speak. Subtextual stimuli arise from the situation and the immediate envi-ronmental circumstances which stimulate the scene. Apply to a spe-cific scene in a play:

• Candida and Morell in Act II. Morell is working on a sermon at his desk, but still ringing in his ears are Eugene's words from their encounter earlier in the day: "I love your wife....I'll fight you with ideas....In her heart she despised her husband...." Morell's stomach twists into knots of doubt, his brow has become clouded with suspicion, his eyes tortured with anxiety.

Candida has been going through the house, putting things in order, helping Maria and Eugene peel potatoes for dinner. She goes to find James, to take care of him; when she enters the study what does she see? James hunched over his dimly-lit desk, his spine sunk a little, his eyes tired, a little stormcloud over his brow. Seeing her overworked husband looking more drawn than usual, she decides to do something that she has often wanted to do: make James realize that his sermonizing is for naught; that his parishioners have little response to his back-breaking labor; that his health is deteriorating because of his workaholic nature.

Candida is ignorant of what has transpired between James and Eugene, so the loving wife and mother goes to her next task: She becomes the loving teacher. What she must do may hurt James a little, but it is time for her to take care of the situation.

What follows is an intimate scene between a husband and wife who have always loved and trusted each other absolutely. Candida installs James in a comfortable chair, sits at his feet where she can rest her head on his lap, where he can feel like the man of the house, and she can be his unthreatening wife. Her idea is to get James as comfortable and secure as possible because she is about to shake the foundation of his life. Her goal is to get James to slow down, mistakenly thinking his harried appearance is due to overwork.

The drama and the comedy come from Candida's ignorance of James' frenzy over Eugene's pronouncements and James' blindness to the utter innocence of Candida's relationship with Eugene. At every moment, James responds to Candida's every sensory stimulus: tone of voice, shift of head, movement of spine. Candida, too, senses some barely perceptible uneasiness beneath James' assured masculine manner as head of the household.

Shaw's brilliant language underscores the real drama of this scene, which depends upon each character's reading and misreading of the multitude of nonverbal stimuli and responses. Each actor must be able to create the situation truthfully and allow her responses to happen naturally rather than acting the way she thinks they would if this situation was really happening.

A constructive way to throw light on a problem is to imagine if it were something else. Discover what is significant about James' study by asking what stimuli Candida and Morell would respond to if they were in the back garden, or in their bedroom. How does "the study" contribute to the full range of stimuli/responses that make up this scene?

• Improvise and describe the dangerous, unspoken sensory interaction between Hedda Gabler and Judge Brack that opens Act II. Create the environment and the situation first as Judge Brack, then as Hedda. Improvise the entire encounter alternately as Brack and Hedda. Describe, moment by moment, the stimuli each responds to and its subsequent effect. Discover why this scene must take place in that parlor by improvising it at a public park picnic table; try it in a veranda bedroom a la *Cat on a Hot Tin Roof*.

Come back to the Ibsen parlor. Is this a situation of simple, harmless sexual innuendo? How is it carrying Hedda one step closer to suicide? What is Hedda responding to besides Judge Brack? Where does the line "You have no idea how mortally bored I have been" come from? What responses to what stimuli have preceded the final eruption of these words into human interaction? Let Hedda see the dark-green flowered pattern in the carpet, the polished dark wood tables, the heavy velvet draperies, the little knick-knacks on shelves everywhere, the curve of the chairback and the little hand-crocheted antimacassar (a gift from Aunt Julie?), the way the light hits that particular vase. Let Hedda hear the grandfather clock out in the hall ticking off the seconds of her life. Let her smell the old oil polish in the floors. It all is playing upon her as she and Judge Brack talk and it is all carrying her along until some one final something touches off the words, "You have no idea how mortally bored I have been, Judge."

Become Judge Brack. Come around the turn in the backyard path and see Hedda standing in the doorway. What exactly does he see? What visual details? With what response? Be specific by actually doing it and discovering. Lead him right into the house. Why must this scene happen here and nowhere else?

Find other examples in drama:

• Take a look at the first few lines of Hamlet's scene with Gertrude. What does she expect Hamlet to say or do in response to her first statement? Be specific, literal in your answer. Note: She begins to prepare herself for that anticipated response just as he fires back at her, catching her off-balance. She recovers (how well?) and responds by firing at him. What does she expect in return?

• In Act II of *Three Sisters*, Masha comments on the wind blowing in the chimney. This is the only time in the scene that a character mentions this stimulus, but it must be present throughout the act. Other characters must respond to it on some subtextual level.

• Everyone responds to the setting sun in Act II of *The Cherry Orchard*. Create the environment and the situation by improvising individual character reponses to specific subtexual stimuli. Note how long Anya and Trofimov must respond to the rising moon at the end of the act before Anya actually says it in words.

• Everyone responds to the powerful reality: 'The Cherry Orchard Is Going to Be Sold' throughout that play. Sensory stimuli carry that meaning to the responses of all characters. Explore each character in each act from the point of view of their subtextual responses to this determining force.

For example:

Varya cleans the house the night before Lubov returns and her actions reveal: The Cherry Orchard Is Going to Be Sold. Before going to the station to greet Lubov, Gaev gets dressed with Fiers' assistance: The Cherry Orchard is Going to Be Sold. Lubov sits and watches the sun going down on the orchard, senses the river behind where his son Grisha drowned.: The Cherry Orchard Is Going To Be Sold. Invent an illustration for Lopakhin.

• Mrs. Alving has lived in her house her entire married life. Was it in this room and on that sofa that the drunken Captain Alving would sleep until dawn? Does Mrs. Alving still stare into the same pattern in the carpet as she did when contemplating her husband's infidelities?

• Create the subtextual sensory environment for the balcony scene of *Romeo and Juliet*. Try Romeo's visit to Friar Laurence's cell. Discover the subtext stimuli at work on the Nurse in her scene with

Juliet after returning from her interview with Romeo. Her feet are aching, the sun is beating down, her stomach growls.

For a while, part of every actor must become the conscious observer/analyzer of the ordinary human being who is experiencing life. This conscious observer/analyzer ultimately becomes an unconscious artist-self doing its job. Study the infinite variations that human beings play on the simple structure of stimulus/response. When you work alone to test your study, recreate significant experiences. Recreate the walk along the harbor with the friend by recreating the stimuli that touched off responses—recreate the meaningful situation through sensory response. Note how frequently specific sensory stimuli have touched off the deepest kinds of associative responses. Notice that the many facets of simultaneous response possess different qualities of associative follow-through/play-through in your whole body.

By "respond" I do not mean the mental abstraction that you afterwards apply to the general situation: "I responded uneasily to his nervousness." Response means concrete, active, physical, sensory phenomena caused by an immediate specific external stimulus with a specific observable physical sensory change, however subtle it may be. Notice, finally, how the phenomenon of a specific stimulus and the specific response it touches off is a single phenomenon, not really comprising separable elements, but existing as a unified organic experience.

Since we are rarely conscious of any but the minutest part of our responses at any one time, when actors must consciously create them, they often distort and destroy reality, focusing too much on the emotional components to do all the work. Actors must become conscious students of human behavior and hoarders of unconscious human responsiveness, for it is from this process that they make a performing art believable, and are communicative on more than simply the most superficial level.

Illustrating Response

1. Students illustrate points made in class about human behavior with recreated moments from their lives: "Oh, I remember

the day I saw my father turn into a kid again when he met his high school football coach after twenty-five years." As the student recreates this encounter for everyone take note of elements of true response:

• Images re-experienced instantaneously before and behind words. (See the section called "Behind the Word" in this chapter.)

• The voice playing opposite to, or even against, the body in response.

• Locate the true secondary importance of "emotion" in the totality of the event. Ask, "Exactly what is happening at this specific time that we label emotion?" Focus attention on the specific nature of the physical response that precedes emotion.

• Look for the several layers of response as they play through in various parts of the body.

2. Other class members recreate on the spot: How much have you truly perceived and stored up of what has been happening in front of you? How much does your actor's self now have to create with?

3. To teach students to look beyond the words, each may ask three "Yes" or "No" questions of the teacher. They must have something they want to find out but they cannot ask directly. It is most effective to have the student's deepest self involved so that they are naturally motivated to have their entire sensory self on alert. Perhaps they are to ascertain just what the teacher thinks of them as students and as actors; perhaps some agreed-upon variation of the old television show, "I've Got a Secret." The teacher will answer only "yes" or "no," which may be the truth or it may be a lie. But the students must sense and respond to everything else the teacher is doing before, during, and after the simple word. By the end of the interrogation, they must know the answer to their unasked question.

Afterwards let students analyze what happened; recreate the discoveries of how human beings interact and communicate.

4. Recreate or invent a charged situation in which you must communicate urgently with another. Both of you must speak in a nonsense foreign language. Take note of how many other clues your totality reads in its attempt to understand and to be understood.

5. Any acting class has moments when a student exhibits an extreme form of behavior. Use these moments to illustrate how absolutely unobjective we all get in significant times of intense response. The objective actor-self is pushed into the background and what usually happens afterward, when we are asked to recreate the situation, is that we "remember" only a few aural and visual images clearly. We concentrate on the general emotional wash of the entire event, rather than the specific interaction of stimuli and responses that actually constituted the experience. It helps to have such moments pointed out so that the objective artist can examine what the subjective person is doing. Actors must train themselves to allow the objective observer and collector to store up what people, including themselves, actually do in highly-charged situations.

6. In individual work and occasionally in class time, recreate a particularly vivid experience: "What was the most interactive event you experienced today?" Recreate it by responding to the particular details that touched you until you have truthfully recreated the experience. Recreate a particularly significant "conversation." Note that the more vivid or profound a "conversation" is, the more important are the responses to the non-verbal aspects. The more important the choice of words is, the more intent you are on being understood. What do you actually do to make certain that understanding is coming across? What are your listeners doing that lets you know whether or not you are succeeding? Pay particular attention to what qualities in the voice you respond to besides the actual denotative words.

7. Tape record a particularly intense conversation or dramatic interchange, one in which you may not be directly involved. Transcribe the tape and give the "dialogue" to your classmates. Let them describe in detail what they think is happening based solely on the transcription. People will be amazed at how difficult it is to get a sense of the total experience purely from the spoken words. What is added when they hear a sound recording of the interaction? What if you recorded the experience on video tape? What would actually having witnessed the event add to a fuller comprehension?

While dramatic dialogue is much more artfully constructed than real conversation, the situations constituting dramatic dialogue are equally charged, equally significant; therefore, the relationship of words to actual experience (in realistic drama) is much the same in both cases. Similarly, while the stimuli that create the subtextual responses in any real life situation may be random, even meaningless, a good playwright orchestrates the influential stimuli of a play to create a pattern of subtext that contributes directly to the cumulatively meaningful experience of the play.

Let's concentrate on issues of response involved in improvisation:

• Consider a highly-charged scene from *The Cherry Orchard*.

Describe what happens between Varya and Lopakhin in Act IV as though it was a situation you witnessed for the above improvisation.

1. Words alone.
2. A sound recording of what happened. (Include "sound effects.")
3. A videotape adds what information? How should you work on these realities and translate them into your acting?

• Try it with highly-verbal playwrights:

Morell and Marchbanks confront each other in Act III.

Lord Capulet confronts Juliet (III, v).

Find ways to respond on many levels of text and subtext:

• Take a favorite soliloquy and as you create Juliet on her balcony, seeing her favorite constellation, sensing the summer night air; look out your window and count the leaves on the branch so that as you say "A rose by any other name...." you can also say "Ten leaves on that branch."

• Try folding a piece of paper, designing paper dolls and cutting them out even as you are completely Juliet responding to her summer Verona garden.

• Move to improvised scenes with more than one person: As you play Trigorin encountering Nina in Act II, work a real crossword puzzle or multiply some number by 13. Play the scene as fully as possible, while simultaneously performing an independent task.

• In the final scene between Mrs. Alving and Oswald, really play the scene as you do a jig-saw puzzle or arrange a box of knick-knacks according to size or color.

When you've got the several levels of your mind working, play scenes by choosing activities appropriate to the character:

• In *Candida*, play the beginning of Act III with Eugene. Page through a pattern book and choose a pattern for a housedress, even as another part of your mind once more hears and sees James telling you to stay at home during the last scene of Act II.

• As Hedda, play the "album scene" with Lovborg, a scene that requires several levels of response (the album, the presence of Brack and Tesman, the immediacy of Lovborg). As you do this, sketch your father, or clean your duelling pistol, or groom a horse. Let a newspaper reporter ask you questions about your relationship with Lovborg as you play the scene. Work to bring into active response the multi-levels at which your mind, your muscles, your brain, your senses, your totality, respond to the world.

You may need to work on the very capacity to respond freely, spontaneously, in the improvisational structure of a scene. Free your senses to respond honestly, truly, when you are on stage:

• As the characters in the play, use the foreign language exercise. Arkadina and Treplev, speak in nonsense Russian as you try to communicate with each other. This will force you to respond to more than just words and scatter-shot emotion. You will discover whether you are creating with totality the entire experience of the scene, or if you are really just trying to motivate and justify the next line.

• Do a "dream version" of what happens so that you are freed from the logic of everyday reality.

• Improvise a similar situation without the dramatic finality of the one scene you work on: On a rare trip to the city, Treplev visits Arkadina back stage. In a tender moment, Arkadina soothes Treplev when a story of his is rejected.

• Let one character actually do what another character is hoping for. When Treplev asks, "Why do you let that man ruin your life?" Arkadina realizes the pain she causes Treplev, she clasps him to her bosom, promises never to hurt him again, asks what she can do to help him. This will give the actor/Treplev the real sensory responses that the person/Treplev is hoping for.

• Work on the scene in which Treplev brings the dead sea gull to Nina and let Nina actually do what Treplev is hoping she will do.

• Work in pantomime.

• Let yourself freeform dance the scene: Is it a Martha Graham scene? (Actors working to embody Greek tragedy would do well to study Graham's several pieces based on Greek myths: look for depth, clarity and passion of motivation, magnitude of expression, vastness of response.) Use the freedom of movement in classical ballet or modern free-flow or jazz to create true responses.

• Imagine that the audience is deaf; play the balcony scene from *Romeo and Juliet* and communicate it, response by response, to the deaf audience.

• Imagine the audience is blind; improvise the seemingly static conversation scene between Hedda and Judge Brack in Act II. Can you communicate to a blind audience the several levels of drama happening in this scene?

These blind and deaf exercises can help you avoid the simple emotional underpinnings actors often mistake for drama. They help actors to discover the drama that animates every scene of a play, exposing the kinesthetic reality inherent in language as it plays beneath even the most static of conversations.

• The act of singing is connected to a part of the brain different from the act of speaking. You must free yourself from conscious intellectual control of what you are doing if you are to be able to sing freely and to respond. Try to create an operatic version of the scene, letting rhythms and melodies play themselves as you respond. And to sing well the player cannot indulge in overemotionalizing: singing is an attempt to put powerful emotions into communication form. Stimulate the communication process on all levels of sensory response.

• The actors behind Hedda and Judge Brack may discover the intricacy and the delight of their dangerous conversation in Act II by literally playing with fire. Who strikes the match first? Discover the excitement of handing a lit match back and forth, each daring the other to let the flame come closer than is safe. When does it turn unpleasant? Who stops the game? Why?

Forget blocking and staging and the concerns of the production rehearsal process. For now, forget lines. Paraphrase. Improvise. Work to create truthfully the experiences you will later cast into form. There is no one right set of exercises to teach or to learn these principles. But if the principles are clear and right, you will begin to ask questions to discover your own speculative examples.

• • •

Learn to visualize dramatic characters in action. What are they actually doing in this scene? Let the play give you clues. What is Friar Laurence doing when Romeo bursts into his life that morning? Think in terms of real people in real environments, responding to real stimuli, performing real tasks. Myriad interactive interplaying stimuli/responses go beyond words when you actually go into a garden one morning to improvise this encounter.

Does Friar Laurence continue his activity once Romeo comes into his garden? If not, why does he stop? What exactly does he hear in tone, brightness, and pitch? What does he see when he looks up? Be specific: Not just "Romeo," not just "a young boy," but specifically and literally, what details? What does he subsequently do? Why?

What is Romeo actually doing? Avoid thinking in generalities such as, wondering whether Friar Laurence will help him, but in actualities: Is he standing? Does he walk about? Does he sit? Where? Why or why not? Does he see the strange little purple herb that Friar Laurence is pruning? Does he see dew sparkling on the flower petals? Are birds singing in the trees? Does he watch the Friar examine the plant he just picked from beneath the old tree trunk? Do they both hear the mourning dove off through the trees? Do they see the other's responses? Do they share it? Do both of them see and respond to sun-and-shadow leaf patterns on each other?

Expand on the intensified quality of the scene with Trigorin and Nina in Act II of *The Sea Gull*. The motivated selves of these people are deeply engaged, even if they do not realize it, so their responses are vivid and electric. (Words such as "vivid" and "electric" never imply "more emotional.") For Nina, this has been the most exciting summer of her life: She is on the verge of making a life's career decision, she has met Trigorin and performed before him and Arkadina. On this particular day, she has experienced the everyday life of famous people, almost swooning with excitement. And then, Trigorin comes toward her, the first time she has encountered him alone all summer. He is taking notes for a short story and her heart leaps with the joy of watching artistic creation firsthand.

Trigorin sees qualities in Nina, youth, vitality, purity of spirit, which he thinks can save him, or restore him to his more promising, vibrant self.

Actors transform these abstractions into specific character responses to specific stimuli. Nina, do you truly see Trigorin's finger grip his pencil? Trigorin, do you really see the life sparkling in Nina's eyes? As you speak, do you see her fingers playing with the lace at her sleeve? As she speaks, do you see and respond to her spine as it lifts up and toward you? Have you seen that cloud long before you point it out in words? Nina, has he gotten sunburnt in the last few days, looking more countrified than at first? Beware: it's easy to fool yourself into thinking that you see when in fact you do not. You "act" as though you see. Result: faked responses, trumped-up emotions, shallow playing, and certain death to true response.

From these never-verbalized responses true drama grows, and the real danger between these two people takes form. Neither of them is actually aware of the danger. Chekhov gives the audience the chance to see the aspiring young actress carried away on a cloud of dreams about theatre as well as the hollow man struggling to regain his life and youth.

Theatre allows us to see the truth that we so often fail to see in our everyday lives. It is life placed before us at an objective distance so that we may truly understand. That experience begins with truthful response manifested in all elements at play in any given situation. Without it, you will respond out of remembered generalized emotional states.

As you analyze your work on specific plays, ask yourself: "Am I truly receiving and responding to stimuli, or am I waiting patiently to deliver my next carefully memorized line? Am I free to respond to stimuli in the environment, or am I so locked to my lines that all I can do is try to justify my next one? Do I really look into eyes and see what's there? Do I read the thoughts behind those eyes? Are my eyes really demanding a response from my partner? Do I artificially maintain eye contact when, in reality, the last place I would be looking is at the person with whom I have created this situation? Do I hear the unspoken? Do I respond to tone? Am I hearing and sensing implication, the hidden, the half-realized, the rejected, the hoped-for, in another person's voice? Or am I too busy trying to feel an emotion until it's my turn to speak?

Do I let words and ideas strike me in the heart, the gut, the mind, and let my responses play through? Do I let myself gasp, reach, try to speak during the other's speech, or am I so very polite to wait until it's my turn to deliver my own words? Are my muscles honestly responding to the tensions, the shifts, the relaxations, the meaning of the spine and muscles of the other character? Or are they merely trying to maintain an emotion or attitude? Busy working up enough emotion to carry me through the other person's speech?

Do you actively pursue your own direct, clear objective of action, or do you simply give your "speeches" with all the emotion you can muster? Do you let yourself respond until you need to speak, to conceal, to escape, to interrupt, to agree, to object, to reinforce, to stifle, to soothe, to reject, or to accept the other person in word, in deed, in totality? Do you let yourself respond to eyes, to muscles, to spine? Do you respond in kind, holding back your words until and unless you have to speak? Words happen when actions are not enough. If you can do anything else, do it. Do not speak a word until there is no choice but to speak, until some part of your body must commandeer the voice to complete the physical response of the moment.

The director counts on the actors' ability to respond to all stimuli in order to select the most significant responses and eliminate others. Friar Laurence, Capulet, Tybalt and the Nurse, as much as Trigorin, Nina and Treplev, must first be real people responding in real everyday ways to real stimuli. Only then can you intensify that reality, alter it, deepen or de-emphasize it, heighten one aspect, or clarify another, into the artistic reality of *Romeo and Juliet* or *The Sea Gull.*

Try this loosely improvised approach to avoid focusing too hard on performance techniques:

- Realism

     1. Outdoors (Anya and Trofimov in Act II of *The Cherry Orchard*)
     2. Indoors (Masha and Trigorin at the beginning of Act III of *The Sea Gull*)

- In Sophocles' *Antigone* what details of environment must Antigone and Ismene respond to in order to create the reality of what happens to them in the first scene? These cannot be the minor details of psychological realism (a pair of spectacles that slip on the nose, the sound of birds scuffling among the branches of a tree, the way the moon casts a shadow on that old stone), but details appropriate to the play: The gates that open to the field where their brother's body lies; the mountain peak where the first rays of the sun will appear; the huge palace door behind them, perhaps the sound of marching boots enclosing the entire space as a way to literalize the reality of "martial law."

Drama draws its lifeblood from true human behavior. Develop the artist's ability to see behind the surface of human behavior. Unlike everyday life, dramatic characters are engaged in situations that activate their deepest motivated selves, not simply their most emotional selves. Responses are heightened and intensified beyond the tepid degree of our daily lives. (It might be depressing to discover how little of each waking day our deepest selves are really engaged in what is happening to us. On the other hand, if we lived as intensely as characters in plays must live, we too would probably burn out in the two hour's traffic of our lives.)

Drama springs from totality and multiplicity of response, not simply from an emotion, however strongly felt, nor from a passionate line, however thrillingly delivered. In realism, the opposition between the inner life and the outer surface events is the drama. The playwright can only furnish a fraction of this totality of response but cannot provide you the complete inner life that plays through the characters. Actors must improvise to touch off these currents until they are alive, playing through, responding habitually and clearly and, yes, unconsciously. The playwright has supplied the words, which constitute the least communicative part of the whole vocal response, which itself is the final part of a total physical response. Learn to read a play and to see the people living, responding, behind the words. Learn to sense situation and to create interactive response, a minor part of which is the vocal response.

If actors focus on the interaction rather than the words or emotions; if actors let the interplay between people take precedence; if actors allow themselves to truly respond to one another and let their spoken words, however brilliant, be only the vocal spark of a total sparkling interaction, then the audience can experience the true interactive human communication which is theatre. Too often actors pretend to respond and then try to inject life into their words because there is, at best, only liveliness in their interactions. Put life in the response and it will carry into the language.

Varying genres of play will manifest these principles with varying degrees of complexity. Realism, especially the great nineteenth-century realists, demands the most intricate version of simultaneous levels at work. But all genres function on this principle regardless of the degree of their realism or irrealism, just as in painting there are principles of light and shadow, of color contrast, of composition, that are adhered to regardless of the degree of realism of the individual painting.

Interplay

Theatre has always built its art on the realities of human interplay. To study interplay from the actor's point of view, we quite naturally turn to real life: How do people interact and what actually happens during "interplay"?

The details of interplay are difficult to observe because they are continually happening, and the moment one becomes aware of them, the process is altered. Still, the actor must make a conscious study of the phenomenon for it is with this very capacity of human interaction that actors communicate to an audience something true about reality. The more crucial the situation, the more important the immediate objectives, the higher the stakes of the interplay, the more dramatic the entire experience becomes.

To illustrate, let us imagine a business meeting. Each person has a motivating drive that is deeply involved in the underlying currents of the meeting: a junior executive knows that if he can get his ideas accepted, it will help him climb the corporate ladder; a conservationist must not let her business make a decision that will jeopardize the environment; someone is having an affair with the spouse of someone else present at the meeting. Responses are acutely heightened and the interplay is intensified. Perhaps a motivated spine may have little to do with any of the forces activated by the meeting, but still it responds. Such interactions, however, do not drive deep; rather they play along the surface without significant engagement of the essential driving force of the individual.

Much of our daily lives is lived in this latter state. Good drama happens in situations of the former.

If we could see a situation like this in black light and if we could paint in color codes the ideas and impulses that were bouncing around, we could tangibly clarify for the actor the complex process of interplay. Add flashes of light for each moment of unverbalized, subtextual depth-charge response that happens in any intensified situation, and you could graphically illustrate yet another layer. Note again, only a small portion of the interactive forces creating interplay at any moment results in actual spoken language.

Improvise a meeting such as the one described above. After twenty minutes or so, let individuals clarify for one another the various threads of interplay that occurred, focusing on moments of true response both verbalized not. Pay particular attention to the manifestations of these interweaving threads of response. What does a perceptive actor observe that reveals each "interplay string"?

Study social functions that activate deep, interlocking, or conflicting currents among people:

- The arrival of a family member from a long journey

- Significant departures for the same

- Important ritual occasions such as anniversaries, funerals, family dinners.

These experiences always touch off the deepest currents of human response, often adequately verbalized.

Each act of Chekhov's plays is built on the determining undercurrents of such occasions. The inevitable destruction of the cherry orchard is the deepest unifying force in that play, and each act particularizes the group's responses during occasions of heightened human interplay:

- Act I—Lubov's arrival in the earliest morning hours

- Act II—A visit to a particularly evocative spot on the estate

- Act III—Lubov's ill-advised party on the evening of the auction

- Act IV—The departure from the estate.

Improvise the situation of each act without focusing on individual scenes or dialogue; rather, concentrate on creating situation and environment and establishing the many subtextual currents of interplay:

1.) As such currents exist in any such situation;
2.) As the currents manifest themselves with particular attention to the specific details of *The Cherry Orchard* people.

For example, the arrival at the family home of a much-loved, long-absent adult animates certain kinds of interplay regardless of who the individuals are. Create this first. Then become more particular: This house is going to have to be sold; Lubov will not be able to save it; Varya has felt dreadful about sending Anya and Charlotta off to get Lubov; and so on.

In *Three Sisters*, each character responds to Natasha's taking over the house while each act is set against a galvanizing experience for all:

- Irina's name-day party

- A traditional Lenten celebration

- A fire in the town

- The departure of the regiment.

The Sea Gull:

- Arkadina's annual summer houseparty

- The day each summer when Arkadina gets so bored that she must escape into town

- Arkadina's departure

- Arkadina returns because Sorin is deathly ill.

The logic of what happens in the plays is the synchronistic logic of response and interplay of real life situations. It is not the linear logic of narrative fiction nor the cause-and-effect dialogue of formal debate, which may account for the frustration many people feel when reading these plays. The stimuli that directly result in verbal interchange in any of these situations make up a very small percentage of the full range of stimuli, touching off individual responses that collectively constitute the interplay of that sequence.

Find real life illustrations to the nature of the interplay between these couples:

- Hedda and Judge Brack, Act II

- Nina and Trigorin, Act II

- Prossy and Marchbanks, Act II.

- The Capulets and Benvolio at the beginning of the play.

Opposites

Since drama, and therefore acting, examines human behavior from the standpoint of conflict and contradiction, actors must develop the ability to see the world in terms of opposites. Can you see yourself in terms of fundamental oppositions and how they express themselves in you? For example:

- The realist who sees the world objectively, even dispassionately as opposed to the romantic whose heart swells with the possibility of "true love"

- The provincial mind inside the body of the world-traveller

• The innocent child huddled inside the big bear of a body.

Hitchcock exploited the sensual woman beneath the ice goddess in Grace Kelly. Marilyn Monroe's appeal was largely based on the perception of the slightly befuddled innocent child inside the sexual woman's body. Didn't Marlon Brando successfully exploit the sensitive soul inside the working class man? Even chameleon actors such as Laurence Olivier and Meryl Streep have their essential opposites. Can you create your version of their opposites?

Look for opposites in others:

• Do you perceive the complacent person beneath the shy words?

• Do you perceive the insecure person beneath the cool exterior?

• What are your father's opposites?

• Have you sensed opposites in your teacher? Illustrate.

• Look at the President of the United States from this perspective.

Try creating these:

• The settled spine with lively sparkling eyes

• The confident forward-going spine betrayed by the meek, apologetic voice.

• The old person who refuses to die

• The concert pianist who gets arthritis in her fingers

• Beethoven goes deaf while composing the "Ninth Symphony"

• A young dancer coming into the street after a performance gets a gun stuck in his back

• The rock star whose spine is broken in an automobile accident

• The prisoner who wants to escape

• The football player who becomes paralyzed

• The peasant who tries to learn refinement of manners

• The kindly, compassionate voice and hands of a young man who has the eyes and spine of a manipulator

• The sensitive, gentle young person with the instinct of the competitive athlete

• The caged, trapped spine of a Hedda hiding itself with a lovely laugh, a lean back into the sofa, a turn of the head

• The vibrant, youthful spine of Romeo facing the reality of banishment.

For every need, every positive response, look for its contradictory pull, the opposite need or response:

• I want to act but I need financial security.

• I want to learn but I fear ridicule.

• I want to work hard but I need to escape my fear of failure by spending time at the movies with my friends.

• I want to—? but I want, need, fear—?

How is each manifested?

Within individual characters:

• Iago's soldier's spine and voice say, "I am honest Iago," but somewhere behind his eyes, somewhere along the muscles that keep the spine erect, the devil of destruction wants to dance as the town burns.

• Hedda is a trapped and caged person inside an aristocratic lady who refuses to give anyone reason to whisper about her.

• Lopakhin: Peasant (Put into action) in conflict with what?

• Macbeth the soldier, defending his king, wants the throne himself.

• What are Marchbanks' opposites?

• What is the opposite of Arkadina's star spine?

What stimuli animate each "self"? Manifested by what specific behavior?

Improvise the opposites inherent in character and environment:

• Arkadina's star-motivated spine (center of attention, throngs of admirers) comes to the country (a wide croquet lawn and Sorin in his wheelchair snores under a tree).

• Lopakhin's wood-chopping peasant spine enters Gaev's house (create specific stimuli).

• Hamlet's trusting son's spine hears his mother's sensual laughter as Claudius puts his arms around her.

Vocal opposites:

• Arkadina's charming, winning voice explodes into Jove's anger; her modulated, well-trained, powerful, commanding voice opposes Nina's naturally lyrical, honest voice.

• Mercutio's poet's voice (lightning quick, scaling the entire vocal range) against Tybalt's (What is the voice of The Prince of Cats?) or Benvolio's (You describe it).

• Trigorin's passion to go deeper into experience counterbalances the dry, shallow celebrity he has become. He sees a sea gull soaring against the sky and his unresponsive muscles simply take note: a sea gull against a blue summer sky. A fish plops in the lake: "Good fishing here," says the writer. Period. Note the drama in the opposition of Trigorin's words: "I love this water here, the trees, the sky, I feel nature, it stirs in me a passion, an irresistible desire to write." The dead voice kinesthetics that are saying them are like an unoiled machine trying desperately to work at its former capacity.

• Morell's resonant minister's voice against Marchbanks' youthful ideological fire

• Treplev as opposed to Nina or Trigorin (What do you discover? Be specific.)

• Romeo counters the Friar

Say one thing, do the opposite:

Assume a position that most fully expresses Grief to you, or Exhilaration, or Victory. With one movement of some part of the body (a lift of the head, an adjustment of the leg,) express this quality. Then, as you express Grief with a physical motion, let your voice say the opposite. Devise variations on this illustration. Look for examples in real life.

Try it with characters:

• In Act IV of *Three Sisters* Olga reveals the whole story as she states straightforwardly, "Things don't always turn out the way we wanted them to. I didn't want to become a Headmistress and now I am one." At the same time she crushes the autumn leaf in her hand.

• What does Treplev do in Act I with the daisy in his hand as he smiles and his voice says lightly, "My mother doesn't understand me"?

• What does Marchbanks' fearful little body do as his eyes and voice attack Morell with the realization, "You are afraid of me"?

• Find such moments for Hamlet, for Hedda, Lopakhin.

Spines

Opposing spines give clues to the source of the drama.

Try studying the currents of a drama through the spines of the characters:

• The heavy spine of Treplev yearning for the power to soar, to release itself in writing opposes the free and soaring spine of Nina longing to sail into the theatre, which in turn counters the actress spine of Arkadina, practiced in its grace, determined to be the center of attention, charming and young forever.

• The free, responsive, vivacious spine of Regina (*Ghosts*) greets the straight, narrow, constrained spine of Pastor Manders.

• The trapped female spine of Hedda comes up against the confident, free male spine of Judge Brack. What is the comedy/drama of the close-minded researcher spine of Tesman as opposed to the confident, outgoing "man-about-town" spine of Judge Brack? Now put in the caged spine of Hedda, longing for release. How does Thea's concerned, hopeful, altruistic spine fit in as an opposite? Where does Lovborg fit in? What clues does Ibsen give you?

Resistance to Forces

Do you love walking against a strong wind? Climbing a hill with exhilaration? Walking up a down escalator? Recreate these actual, literal opposing forces as a way to discover how such opposition feels and what muscles are involved. Can you then recreate times when forces were playing upon you metaphorically? When you felt the whole weight of the world on your shoulders? When you were up against a wall? When, like Alice's Red Queen, you felt as though you were running fast just to stay in one place? Add more examples. Do them all. What do you discover about the drama inherent in resistance to forces?

Literalize Masha in *The Sea Gull* when she says she feels as if she were dragging her life behind her like the endless train of a dress. What implications do you discover for her total response to life? In a well-received production recently, Masha entered in Act I with a swing of her hips and a slight bounce to her walk. As Medvedenko began to talk, she threw herself carelessly onto the ground and lolled about, pulling flowers and rolling her eyes in disgust. When she spoke the line about the train in Act II, it came as an over-dramatizing lie rather than a simple statement of truth. Perhaps it is simply a question of interpretation, but other clues in the play give more weight to one choice over another. For example, people who are close to such self-dramatizing others tend to talk about them when they leave the group, as Masha does in Act II. Note what is said about her in this event. Why? What is revealed here? Identify and clarify other clues the play gives to Masha's character.

In partners:

• One stands behind the other, with hands on the front person's shoulders. At a signal both start to pull: the front person, moving from the pelvis, takes a strong, slow step forward as the back person, initiating from the pelvis pulls back on the front person's shoulders. They perform these opposite pulls not in competition, but in concert until they sense a moment when the forces have reached a peak and then they snap apart: the front person concludes the step forward with gusto and the back person springs with follow-through.

• The front person now tries the same thing imagining the swing of a heavy velvet cape as the positive force that pulls down on shoulders. Play variations on these opposing forces in twos and threes. The goal is to experience vividly the nature of resistance to forces. This aspect of movement should be present at every moment on stage. A character doesn't simply sit in a chair: There are forces to be resisted, overcome, tiny body decisions to be made with every movement on stage. The possibility of following any one of the several forces at work on the human being at any given moment is a source of drama and suspense.

Apply this idea as:

• Prince Hal lifts the King's crown and puts it on his head

• Cleopatra puts on her crown and her robe.

• Hedda opens the case and takes out a pistol.

The absence of such opposition in supernumeraries can absolutely kill the suspense of a large scene, even if the principal actors are creating beautifully. Spear-carriers, tomb-bearers, guards and crowds must always keep possibility in their bodies and never get set in one position. Kinesthetically, the whole stage must be communicating possibility and opposition to an audience.

Gravity

The essential force we oppose at all times is gravity as it pulls us toward the center of the earth. How and where we resist gravity in our bodies is a key to character, to motivation, to attitude toward life, toward our sense of the future, even toward basic philosophy of life. Where is the so-called "center of gravity" in a person? Why? What does this say to you about him? Find out by letting your own lower back, your own "center of gravity" assume his and become the natural way you respond.

What is your habitual relationship with gravity? How does it express itself? Note how this can temporarily change: on days when you are so tired that you can barely drag yourself upstairs, a bed or a sofa actually seems to pull you into it. During moments of liberating joy, note your opposite response. Look for people whose habitual responses are like your temporary ones. As an actor you will need to activate your capacities for response so you can transfer them to the center of your being as habitual patterns. They will then help your behavior to be true and motivated, rather than merely assumed or imitated. Fakery is the body's deep awareness that it does not really believe in this kind of behavior, so it just imitates it; if it is trained to sense behavior truly and to improvise until the experience is real, then it has no need to cling to its own private patterns as the only ones that are truly motivated.

• At the clap of the leader's hands, drop to the floor, give in to gravity. At the next clap, spring to your feet in one even motion; do this several times.

• Then: slow motion. Become aware of the source of movement.

• Then: Leader claps and you arrest in mid-movement. Sense how the big muscles of the lower spine are always involved with the initiation of movement and in the dynamic process of balance. (Note what happens in this exercise as people get older, as they lose the ability to resist gravity easily.)

Create from standpoint of resistance to gravity:

• Arkadina (See the beginning of Act II for clues)

• Nina Act I ("I'm drawn to this lake like a sea gull.")

• Nina Act IV

• Juliet's Nurse as opposed to Juliet

• Hamlet's progress though the play from this standpoint

• Try Macbeth, Romeo, King Lear

• Hedda, Judge Brack, and Tesman in opposition to each other.

The curtain goes up on the opening of Act I of *Three Sisters*. On stage are the three sisters. What do we learn about them from their relationship to gravity as it is displayed for us to compare? (Why does Chekhov put all three on stage at once? Why not introduce them one at a time?) Of the three Olga faces life directly, has a solid working relationship with gravity. She simply resists gravity with no great effort but as a matter of course. It's part of facing each day as it comes. (At the end of a hard day at school, the battle is harder fought, though she will resist to her last breath.) Why does she get headaches? Her feet are planted on the ground, her pelvis is in line, her spine lifted, shoulders square, head balanced firmly. (Perhaps a slight turn up and away in the shoulders as she allows herself to daydream about Moscow.) What clues does this description offer for the sound and register of her voice? What is the aim of her ideas? Is that opening speech wistful? Is it a surprise to her? Is she just now realizing these thoughts? Not at all. She states the ideas directly and forcefully. "Last year father died and I thought we would all fall apart. This year we are celebrating a name-day party." Note the change in her by Act II. Look at the confrontation with Natasha in Act III from this perspective.

Note the ease and the joyful, even playful, resistance to gravity that is Irina at the beginning of the play. Compare her relationship to gravity with Olga's. How is this expressed in spine and kinesthetic response? Follow Irina through each act simply by the change in her spine and kinesthetic resistance to gravity. Draw her spine in each act, describing her relationship with gravity in each, accounting for the changes. Note the resulting change in her voice.

How does the way Masha sits at the beginning of the play tell you that she resists gravity neither with joy nor with defeat, but simply as a part of her lot? This woman will not take to drink, as does her namesake in *The Sea Gull*, nor will she become one of the quietly neurotic women of unhappy Victorian marriages. How does she reveal this in her response to gravity? When she enters in Act II, there is music in her walk, joy in her resistance to gravity, a kinesthetic delight in the movement of her skirts, in the feel of snowflakes on her eyelashes. What has happened to her?

Follow Natasha through each act from the point of view of your relationship.

Human Relationships

For the actor, the term "relationship" must be manifested in literal human behavior. Psychologizing, adjectival descriptions, and emotional generalizations, are to be replaced with actual motivated behavior that illustrates any intellectual concept. How can you tell, when you look at an older man and a younger woman, that they are father and daughter? (This reality needn't be biological or literal.) What clues suggest that they are employer and employee, or lovers, or brother and sister? (Notice what is involved when your perception turns out to be wrong.)

What specific objects, activities, and responses, illustrate your relationship to some particular person? What would you suggest an actor who is portraying this relationship do in order to truly create with understanding?

How is your relationship with your mother expressed in spine? Be specific; improvise to illustrate. What does your mother's voice do that expresses her relationship with you? How are relationships expressed through eyes, walk, movement patterns, touch, and other kinesthetic sensory manifestations?

Imagine spines painted to glow in black light. How would this reveal your relationship with your lover, your lawyer, or your minister?

Try the idea that if you had a three-minute video tape to typify your relationship with your father, your best friend, your doctor, what would each of you be doing? Describe in specific terms of illustrative interaction. Improvise to discover.

Then apply to characters:

• Become Hamlet and illustrate his relationship with Gertrude, Ophelia, and Horatio. Draw two lines on a sheet of paper to illustrate each relationship.

• Oppose Nora Helmer's "blacklight" spine for her first scene with Torvald in *A Doll House* and then with Torvald at the end of the play.

• Apply this approach to drama by creating through improvisation, the Arkadina/Trigorin relationship. What clues does Chekhov give you? Have you seen this relationship in real life? A bright, beautiful star is chaperoned by a slightly younger successful handsome man, who is not quite as charming as she, not as effervescent, never going to steal the spotlight. Not to mention the possibility of great sex. Can you see why Arkadina would want or need a

Trigorin? Find photos from the fifties of Elizabeth Taylor and Eddie Fisher. In Act III, when Trigorin says, "I am a weak, spineless man. How can a woman like that?" let yourself discover Arkadina's response.

Try Arkadina and Trigorin at the opening night reception for his new play starring You-know-who. On the train to the summer house, a fan asks for Arkadina's autograph and then recognizes Trigorin. Let Arkadina's response to Nina's introduction to Trigorin in Act I give you clues to behavior.

• Improvise Arkadina's arrival for the summer vacation. Shamraev has allowed several of the locals to gather on the front veranda to welcome her. Treplev asks her to read his play.

• Where are you likely to find the boorish man/stifled woman as seen in the Shamraev/Polina relationship?

• Look for the trapped woman/blind-attentive husband found in the Hedda/Tesman relationship. Describe it in terms of active/reactive spines.

• Tesman has a relationship with Judge Brack. Create it through improvisation. What do you discover?

• Create a few "video bytes" to illustrate the relationship between Candida and Prossy.

• Try this with the characters from *Romeo and Juliet*.

Realizations and Decisions

To the actor, realization is a fundamental building block of drama, for when a character makes a realization, the audience is invited to realize as well. Thus, realization communicates drama directly to the audience. The progress of a play is mapped out by its characters from one major realization to the next until the great climactic realization that ends the play. Restoration and eighteenth-century comedies and nineteenth-century sentimental comedies assemble the entire cast for the climactic revelation of a young person's actual birth—parodied beautifully by Wilde at the end of *The Importance of Being Earnest.* This group realization, when done well, always brings down the house.

We can illustrate from the plays discussed in this book. Work on the following:

• Treplev comes to a realization in his scene with Nina that leads him to put a bullet through his brain.

• Follow the Realization Trail through *Candida* by which Marchbanks comes to his climactic understanding of the place of the poet in the world.

• The entire progress of *Hedda Gabler* leads to Hedda's offstage realization just before she puts the pistol to her head.

• Look for Romeo's and Juliet's major realizations during the course of their play.

What exactly happens during the process of realization? One is struck by a stimulus that astonishes (A-ston-ish-ment means to be struck senseless, to as by a stone). Metaphorically, it strikes you, there is a momentary arrest, and the greater the shock, the more total the arrest. As the jolt travels from the point of impact to your brain, as the energy moves through your heart to strike that clear bell of understanding in your mind, to light that bright light of instant comprehension behind your eyes, you may verbalize what you are realizing or you may be silent. The greater the impact, the longer the journey, the more significant the realization, the clearer the bell, the brighter the light.

To illustrate: You are rushing down the street to catch the last train home, when your hand goes to your back pocket. Suddenly, you realize that you do not have your wallet and the electricity travels instantly to your brain. The body must be arrested in its action in order to allow the biochemical process of realization to happen. Part of you still wants to get your feet running to the train, part of you is stopped cold using a hand to search the rest of your pockets, part of you is thinking of where you have come from and is getting your muscles ready to move back in that direction. In a moment, one or another of these competing forces will take command of your body; you will come to a decision and take action. ("Hell with it, catching the train is most important," or, "I must have that wallet—I'll retrace my steps," or—"Aha! I remember now, I set it down at the restaurant! I can see it in my mind.") The process is the same for every realization; the intensity of each step is dependent on the significance of the realization to your life:

  1) You are in action and
  2.) A stimulus strikes some part of you and
  3.) Arrests your movement to some degree depending on the strength of the impact of the stimulus and
  4.) A flash travels to your brain and a lightbulb goes off which leads you to
  5.) Make a decision that results in
  6.) Action of some sort.

We can visualize the process by using an old carnival game. The hammer (stimulus) strikes the platform (your heart, guts, sense of confidence, etc.), sending the weight (electro-chemo-muscular-neuro energy pathway) upward to strike the bell (moment of intellectual grasp often signified when hand strikes forehead Boing! or Eureka! or Lightbulb!). Then: Decision and action.

At Theatre Arts U. Donna is a student who, when she was thirteen years old, had discovered her mother dead from carbon monoxide poisoning in the car in the garage. She had loved her mother. They were a deeply-religious Roman Catholic family. While Donna was a student in my class, her father had remarried a woman Donna did not like. Donna escaped into memories of her relationship with her mother as warm, safe and lovely. She always wished she had been able to ask her mother why she had killed herself.

Before class one day I asked her if I might tap into these experiences in class to illustrate the process of realization and decision. She agreed. In class I suggested to Donna that her mother was sitting in the lobby outside the classroom. She had been granted a few minutes to come and visit, and Donna could go to see her. Donna's spine lifted with wonder, her eyes went large and bright with joy. She stood still wrapped in wonder, and began to walk to the theatre door. As her hand reached for the knob, I called her name.

She arrested, her hand on the knob and she turned to look at me. "If you go out that door," I said, "you will never be able to return to this class again. If you open that door, you must give up acting and the theatre forever."

The two most powerful Donnas were activated: Donna the child, who loved her mother and who wanted to ask her mother why, was compelled to open the door and go to see her; Donna the actress, the student who imagined her future in the theatre, fought to return to her place in class. The immediate result was total arrested movement. The realization and decision process took a long time. We watched as each Donna gave in to the other and then resisted. At last she looked long at me and the class, her spine straightened with resolve, her hand dropped from the door, a decision was made by the whole organism, and the process was completed by the resultant action taken as she returned to her seat in the class.

Analysis of such a complex moment of arrest, realization, decision, action, reveals that the process of decision-making is not exclusively, or even primarily, an intellectual one. You can begin to see the forces at work on separate parts of a being, in a sense, momentarily commandeering Donna's arms, her need to communicate with her mother as it coursed through her spine and her heart and her eyes. At the same time, part of that spine was commandeered by the committed student of theatre; there was muscular energy holding back the hand that wanted to visit with mother. Yes, the intellect was furiously at work, but it was doing only a fraction of the total process and perhaps not the most significant fraction.

When people speak as they are making realizations, something happens to their voices. In class, a spine will lift, eyes will open, a jaw drop. Still in the wonder of it, and without readjusting spine or where she is in her moment, Eva says, "I just realized something," and her voice does not come from the objective descriptive self that may have been speaking only a moment earlier and that will speak again when the moment has passed. It is possible that, in a millisecond, she will snap completely into the present and her voice will assume a clarity and passion as she explains, "I just realized by watching Treplev with Arkadina why my brother and my mother never get along." But it is just as possible that the impact of the realization will be so great that she will have to stay in that space as she speaks what might be exactly the same words, in which case she is still having a realization and it is still travelling through her (the metal weight is still racing up the column to the bell): "I just realized by watching Treplev with Arkadina why my brother and my mother never get along." Word by word the glow of realization gets brighter, even in the voice. Often there is a pause after such statements to allow the vibrating realizations a chance to strike home and make sense.

While you focus your life-study time on observing and perceiving the phenomena of realization and decision-making, recreate interesting, illustrative moments you have observed in your self and in others. Avoid mere brain comprehension; always give your totality the time to explore and discover. Then ask, "Does this experience have a parallel somewhere in drama?" Then improvise the moment.

• Create Hamlet as he races through the hallway on his way to his mother's closet and suddenly he comes upon Claudius: Realization! "Now could I do it pat!" He's kneeling, his hands are folded: Realization! He's praying!

What decision does Hamlet make? Why? What forces are at work? Why does one win out over the other? How are they manifested? Why are they expressed this way? Action: He slips his rapier back into his belt. What do you reveal about Hamlet at each moment through sensory response? Finally, he takes off for Gertrude's room.

• Greek tragedy contains some of the starkest realizations in all of Western drama. One of the longest tragic realizations happens in Sophocles' *Electra* as Orestes gradually realizes that the filthy savage thing before him, cradling the urn, lamenting, revealing fact upon unbelievable fact about the abuse she has suffered, is in fact his sister, the princess Electra. It takes watching and listening all through her lamentation over the urn for him to come to that realization and to be able to take consequent action.

• *Oedipus Rex* dramatizes responses that lead to a world-shattering realization: Not only is Oedipus the murderer he seeks, but in the very defining experiences of his life, he has violated essential natural laws. Olivier's famous Oedipus animal howl at the climax of his realization stopped time and cracked the vault of the heavens as the tragic dimension of his realization struck him and the audience.

Too often, actors eliminate moments of realization in plays, especially moments of prolonged realization during which characters speak; that is, when characters try to put into fallible, puny words the enormous realization that is overwhelming them. Actors often substitute empty emotionalizing for actual in-the-moment realizing; however convincing such emotion is, the audience must sit passively and be told how a character feels after the realization has happened. How much more dramatic and how much more engaging if the audience has the opportunity to experience the realization along with a character with total sensory participation. And how much more powerfully emotional that is.

• Actresses playing Shaw's Saint Joan in her response to the court in Scene VI, often deliver their "Perpetual imprisonment! Am I not then to be set free?" speech as a righteously indignant or angry or merely petulant outburst. As such, it is essentially undramatic and much too long. It is also difficult to accept that no one in the courtroom attempts to stop her outburst.

But what happens if this long "speech" occurs as part of Joan's coming to a most amazing realization? "My voices were right....They told me you were fools," then becomes not an ugly epithet hurled at God's representatives on earth, but rather an astonishing realization to which Joan must try to put words in order fully to comprehend its impact in a growing series of ever-more-astonishing realizations. The speech becomes the verbal expression of the realization to which the entire play has been leading; it must be given the time and words in which to happen if the realization is indeed to be worthy of its place in the play. Decision and action follow, and the play moves to its final climactic question: "O God that madest this beautiful earth, when will it be ready to receive Thy saints: How long, O Lord, how long?"

• Another scene from drama that is often done with overwrought emotion or with arid intellect to little dramatic point is the confrontation in the jail between Isabella and Claudio in *Measure for Measure*. If Isabella immediately realizes the import of what Claudio has said in his "Ay, but to die, and go we know not where" speech (which itself is a realization on his part) and then spends the next minutes hurling angry abuse at him, or rattling off intellectual rationales, the audience will never grasp how important to Isabella is her own realization.

• The articulation of a realization that is taking place needn't happen instantaneously, nor only during long speeches; it can happen in the course of conversation. Mrs. Alving, in the last scene of *Ghosts*, illustrates this point well. Her actions and words usually come from some generalized well of maternal love expressed alternately as anger, as smothering concern, blindness to Oswald's situation, or scorn for his appreciating neither her nor his father. But if what is happening to Mrs. Alving is a gradual, forceful, horrifying series of realizations, then the drama is focused on what she is realizing (and also, incidentally, on what the play has been dramatizing) rather than just what she and Oswald are feeling.

Of course, emotion does play its part in the total experience. If a person is truly responding to the significant stimuli of a dramatic situation, emotion will be present in the same way that heat and sparks will be present when stone strikes flint. Emotion is a result of the conflict of motivated forces within a person rather than the immediate cause of that person's behavior. It is one of the payoffs of drama, but it is not the source of drama. Shaw suggests that Joan rises "in consternation and terrible anger" before she speaks, but this does not mean that she must utter consternated and terribly angry words, nor even speak only from anger and consternation. Words imply that a person is trying to communicate beyond emotion, so Joan may rise in terrible anger, but her words express the great realization her human totality is experiencing.

Realizations and decisions are physical, sensory, total, not simply intellectual or emotional experiences. As you observe yourself, ask what forces playing upon you clash in what realization that precedes what decision. How do you reveal your character in consequent action?

Work to experience exact moments by when these happen:

• Romeo decides to scale the orchard wall.

• Morell decides to leave Candida with Marchbanks at the end of Act II.

• Hedda decides to give Judge Brack the pistol.

• Hedda decides to pinch Aunt Julie with a comment about her hat. (Why does she need to hear Aunt Julie squeal?)

• Masha (*Three Sisters*) decides to stay to lunch, and she takes off her hat.

• Blanche Dubois decides to seduce the delivery boy.

• Mercutio realizes he is dying and decides to do—what?

• Lopakhin realizes simultaneously that the orchard is his and that he has hurt the person who means the most to him. .

• Mrs. Alving realizes that Oswald has no "blood-love" for his father.

• Marchbanks realizes that Morell is truly afraid of him.

• After making his realization about the place of the poet in society, Marchbanks decides to leave Candida and James and the hearth.

• Macbeth realizes that he will not kill Duncan.

• Hedda realizes that Thea actually left her husband. Over how many lines of dialogue does this realization occur?

• Candida gets Marchbanks to realize something as they sit before the fireplace in the beginning scene of Act III. What is that realization? When exactly does it happen? By what process of smaller realizations and decisions?

• Arkadina decides to change Treplev's bandage.

• Candida realizes that James is not aware of what part she actually plays in the creation of their household.

• Lady Macbeth decides to call on every evil force in the universe to give her the strength to commit murder.

• Plot the series of realizations that Mrs. Alving must make during her last scene with Oswald leading to her final decision.

Try offstage realizations and decisions that directly affect the creation of character and/or the forward progress of the onstage drama:

• Treplev decides to kill a sea gull, a beautiful living thing, when he has not the slightest innate impulse to do such a thing. Why does he take a rifle with him that day?

• Hedda realizes she is twenty nine years old and she decides to let Tesman walk her home from the party. What was Judge Brack doing at that party? With whom did he leave?

If actors respond to the significant and meaningful stimuli in their environment, responding truly to others and to the situation; if they allow realizations and decisions to happen; then the emotional aspects of such interactions will occur of themselves, rather than as manufactured bolsterers to long speeches or rapid-fire interchanges. Possibilities, alternatives, realizations, decisions are what make drama. And it is in moments of drama that meaningful experience is communicated to an audience.

Behind the Word

Behind the word is the image. Behind the image is the experience that is burned into the muscles and the sensory organs so vividly that a word or a phrase in a text touches off the ability to relive it. It instantly flashes across your face, into your fingertips and through your heart, even as the words are being spoken. For example, I was driving the family's only car, a silver-and-gray '57 Chevy Impala, for only the second time since getting my driver's license. I came to a stop behind another car. I looked both ways. The car in front of me pulled away. I again looked to my left, no cars, I stepped on the gas and looked ahead of me. The car in front of me had again come to a full stop.

And now I re-see that immobile green car through my windshield. My foot goes for the brakes as the tires screech. I hit the car with a crunch of metal and I am catapulted into the steering wheel as the hood buckles up toward the windshield like an accordion. Then I slam back into the seat, my heart racing, my sweaty hands clutching the steering wheel.

In an instant I re-experience all those responses as my inarticulate tongue says "I had an accident." Behind that word "accident" is the image, which comprises those detailed responses, and behind them is the actual experience that I stored up so vividly in my being.

Images create the reality that shape and sustain words. Discover the significant images, associations, and thematic metaphors playwrights use. Discover the experiences that you can bring to re-create these words. For instance, "blood," "murder," and "darkness" are words that play throughout Macbeth. What experience will you bring to these words so that they do not remain merely words said with hollow emotion and a beautiful voice but so that they become the vocal part of a truly re-experienced image? Words like "murder" needn't be literal in order to be murder. It is true that, as the famous example goes, "You don't have to have actually committed murder to play Macbeth. Haven't you ever wanted to murder someone?" But "murder" means more than literal physical killing. I have watched professors delight in murdering the career of a colleague by the actions they take during reappointment or tenure reviews. I have experienced the murder of creativity in students by a particularly ruthless teacher/director: I re-hear him say, "Just do what I tell you. Do what I say. We'll have beautiful pictures. This will be a definitive production." His precise oily voice strikes at my spine, my heart, and I cringe. "My production, my interpretation." I see his mirthless smile, watch his fingers play with the knob of his cane as he speaks. The murder of creativity is happening there just as surely as the murder of a person by a bullet fired into a brain or a dagger plunged into a heart. By re-living these detailed stimuli responses, I bring the word "murder" alive in me, re-experience murder in a flash before the vocalization of the word, which may finally come out as pure understatement playing against the experience of the reality of murder.

Work to discover details of response, vividly experienced, deeply stored up that you will put behind these words and lines:

• "Stars," "night," "sky" run throughout *Romeo and Juliet*. What experiences do you bring to each of these words so that they can literally be brought "to life"?

• Jealousy, especially sexual jealousy, can be the most vicious, most destructive, of human passions. Jealousy motivates both the tragic action of *Othello* and the comedy of *A Midsummer-Night's Dream*. Discover and re-create in specific, re-experienced terms, the reality you put behind "jealousy." "O, beware, my lord, of jealousy!

It is the green-eyed monster, which doth mock the meat it feeds on...." and "These are the forgeries of jealousy...."

• "The rest is silence." What is that "silence" of Hamlet? Is there a silence greater than Hamlet's? (Perhaps Treplev's, as he slowly destroys his writing before he leaves to shoot himself in Act IV.) What image do you put behind that single word, that will play beyond it to infinity?

• When I encounter Sophocles' Antigone saying, "There is a greater law than yours," I see my sister's eyes looking directly at me. I see her hands turning over her hospital identification badge. While she was a nurse, the new doctor on the floor ordered her to give a patient medication which she knew might kill him. She told the doctor. His response: "I am the doctor here. I will tell you the diagnosis. You will carry out my orders." She refused. Another nurse gave the medication and the patient died. My sister quit nursing. "There is a law greater than yours."

• "You must listen to reason." What true experience, vividly lived, deeply stored-up, will you bring to Haemon as he faces his father, so that the audience will resonate with the need for reason in this world, rather than just a whining son pleading with his inflexible father? Perhaps you can find stimulation in world events: The homeless in America balanced against the millions spent on developing a new toilet for the space shuttle.

• "Death" is a theme running throughout drama. What is death or nothing-ness for you? Perhaps you have experienced actual physical death, but "Death" need not be so. No more...silence...a door closed forever. As a twenty-four year old, I was teaching high school on the West Side of Chicago. Many of the students, some of whom were placed in the school for disciplinary reasons, came to school everyday on drugs. Willie was the largest sixteen-year old I have ever seen. "Don't bother trying to teach Willie," I was told by the Christian Brothers who ran the school. "We just pass him along, just so he keeps quiet and doesn't disturb the class."

Something in me rebelled against such advice. I was determined to teach Willie. The first semester, grades came out, report cards were placed on each student's desk. Willie came into homeroom late, lumbered to his seat, eyes glassy, mumbling to himself. He heaved himself into the desk that was too small for him, opened his report card. I had given him an "F."

As I tried to conduct homeroom business, I heard Willie mumbling "Sonofabitch, that motherfucker...goddamn..." Everybody sat stark still as Willie heaved himself out of his chair and lurched toward the front of the room. My breath caught in my throat as I imagined the huge and powerful Willie smashing me in the face with his fist for giving him an F. He pushed past me and barged into the hall. His little friend Delmar, the brightest boy in the class, said, "Mr. Downs, maybe I better see what's up with Willie." He scurried out of the room. The class and the teacher held their collective breath. At last Delmar poked his head in the door: "Mr. Downs, Willie wants to see you out by the lockers." The class gasped, looked at each other. My heart beat madly. There was a giggle from somewhere in the room. In that instant, I tried to decide what to do as the class watched me. Do I call security? Do I face Willie? Do I run? Finally, I took a deep breath and went out into the hall.

At the end of the hall, there was the hulking Willie Lee leaning up against the lockers, breathing hard. As I walked toward him, he seemed to get bigger. At last I was beside him. He was mumbling. What to do next? I lifted an arm and put it on his shoulder, the first time I had ever touched Willie. "What's up Willie?"

He shifted his feet, turned to look at me. A beat. Then, "You're a good guy, Mr. Downs. I'm gonna work hard and learn this semester." And he moved past me and went back into the room.

Willie began to write a play that semester. Everyday he brought me a new scene: "Willie Saves His Friends in Nam," "Willie on the Street," "Willie and the Blackstone Rangers." Willie became one of the best students I had. It was one of the most amazing experiences I have had in teaching, and it will never happen again. When I need to put a reality behind that awful word "death," I relive in an instant that glorious moment with Willie, letting myself realize that I will never again experience such a moment.

It is in the re-experienced truthful happening behind the lines (not simply in some emotional response to the idea of that experience) that you will bring human truth to your acting and turn facts, statements, lines, into human drama. As we have illustrated, the re-experienced happening needn't be literal.

• What do you bring to Lady Macbeth's, "My hands are of your color, though I shame to wear a heart so white?" It is not necessary to have steeped you hands in actual blood: "You know how chicken blood feels on your hands, don't you? sticky, wet? Well, you don't need to actually kill someone to know what blood on Lady Macbeth's hands feels like." While this kind of re-living might be part of the total experience, it is imagining on the shallowest level of meaning. The blood on Lady Macbeth's hands is more than sticky wet fluid. What deep, meaningful, accurate, experience do you put behind "My hands are of your color, though I shame to wear a heart so white."?

• Once during an argument my aunt slapped her daughter with such ferocity that the daughter lost her balance. I shall never forget the look on my cousin's face and the horrible pain that stabbed through my aunt as she saw her daughter stagger against the wall. Her hands hung out in front of her, the dread of what she had done clinging to them. She begged her daughter to forgive her.

With that image burned into my muscles and senses, it doesn't take too great a leap of imagination for me to look at my hands, wringing them, trying to rub the experience of that strike out of them as I moan, "Out, damned spot! Out I say."

• Several weeks after my sister died, my mother was holding a photo of her in her hands. She touched the photo gently with fingertips, looked at it, crying, her fingers playing along the features, simultaneously trying to will the life back and to accept that the life was over. "I'll never see her again," she said. And then the following words, each an attempt to comprehend in her muscles the meaning of the word: "Never... never... never... never... ever." My mother did not know *King Lear*, but in that moment, as her fingers tried to put life into the lifeless photo, as her eyes searched the photo for some flicker, as her spine bent in and all her maternal energy tried to bring her daughter back, as her tongue tried to help her totality to realize that the life was gone, to comprehend "Never" (one of the most astonishing attempts to reach full realization I have ever witnessed), she answered the questions about the meaning and delivery of Lear's famous line in a way more exquisitely compelling than any I have read about or seen on the stage.

• Working on the messenger in *Medea* a student actor recreated a high school trip onto a lake with a friend. The outboard motor burst into flames and his friend suffered burns as the student cringed at the other side of the boat, trying to help, screaming, watching, smelling. At the height of his re-creation of the experience in class, he became the messenger in *Medea*, seeing the Princess put the crown on her head, smelling her flesh burn, hearing the screams pierce his ears. Suddenly, confronting Medea, who compelled him to tell his story, the messenger came alive. It was no longer a speech to be memorized, emotionalized and delivered. There aren't words enough to describe the horror and everything in him fights to keep from having to describe it, yet the driving need—"Medea, get out of here"—forces him to go on.

Note that "image" doesn't mean just a "visual picture on the movie screen at the back of your head," but rather, action images, response images, muscle-experienced, sensory-experienced images re-experienced the instant before the tongue finds a word for them. The messenger looks at Medea and the instant before he says "she was so happy," sees again the princess' smile, hears her laughter as the diadem is placed on her head, and instantly sees the twisted face, hears the agonized screams. We see the image instantly flash across his face, into his eyes, into his muscles. Then, "She was so happy."

While the images are re-lived, the character responds to the immediate stimuli of the present. Though the messenger's words may say how happy he and the other servants were, his body is wrenching with the experienced images of brutal violent death and his urgent need to get Medea to leave at once. He is seeing Medea's blazing eyes, hearing Medea's laughter, feeling the heat of the sun as it reflects from the palace stairs.

Study yourself. You see a hand touch a wine glass and as you smile, answer a question, pick up a fork, your body plays through associations from past experience which may or may not find their way to surface external or vocal expression. The mind and the body respond, think and live on many simultaneous planes. In Greek drama, these planes are the most simple. Only those responses and images ("inner life") that directly relate to the immediate action of the drama and which contribute directly to the theme of the drama are created. But truly created they must be, if we are to avoid either those strange, distant Greeks who marched around stage sighing and wailing and chanting continuously, or a contemporary neurotic minimizing of tragedy.

"Re-experience" and "re-live" do not mean "remember." Memory is passive and drama must be active in the present, not in the past. Re-live, re-experience now, in the present, as the responses to immediate stimuli carry you and the drama forward. In a sense remembering is emotion and as such emotion is always passive. I re-see the sunlight slanting in the barred window. I re-hear the calm detached voice. Only certain words ring clear: "The students like you." The pencil taps on his neat, well-organized desk. "...not a very good teacher then...." The sign stands on his desk in perfect white letters: PRINCIPAL. Behind him a wall of books— *Educational Psychology...English Literature in the Secondary Schools.* "...complaints that Willie is working on your assignments in other classes...." My spine tenses, my heart beats faster as I sense what is coming. In the outer office a phone rings. In the hall Delmar's laughter, running footsteps. And the voice continues, "...contract terminated...." As I sit here now re-seeing his hands, re-hearing the tapping pencil and that stark, sterile voice, my heart begins to beat fast, my hands grip the chair and I re-experience that day. I may put words such as "I felt fury, I felt anger, I was taken aback, sick to my stomach," but re-experiencing the stimuli lets me relive the moment actively, in the present, and to bring that specific and instantaneously experienced image (rather than a general emotion) to a word or a phrase in a play that might touch it off.

How does this apply to so-called "memory speeches," such as Blanche DuBois' description to Mitch of her marriage?

Note well the differences between this kind of work and what is usually meant by "emotional recall" or "affective memory" and "substitution." This is not asking the actor to remember how she felt when her dog died so that she can feel grief again; nor is it responding to specific stimuli in order to elicit emotion so that the carry-over into the character and the situation will be the emotional content of the relived situation. The objective of this work is to relive a situation in which significant stimuli and responses may play beneath the words and the ideas of the play to create depth of experience rather than shallow emotional wash.

Even so, while this approach is vital for the process of discovery, it is not intended for performance. This work is part of the early study of the play, part of your own work to bring depth to your creating. As you move further along in rehearsal, becoming more alive to the specific details of the life of the character, the world of the play, and the specific events of each scene, this early work subsides, becomes unconscious, part of the life-stuff which the play puts into form. As you perform the messenger from *Antigone*, or *Medea*, it will be he who experiences his own images, not some schizophrenic mixture of you and him battling simultaneously to create the reality of the play and the truth of any one moment in it. There will be plenty of work left to transform all of this discovery truthfully into the messenger in his particular situation for the thematic ends of the play.

Relive, improvisationally, experiences to put behind these words:

• Hedda: "I really had danced myself out, Judge. My time was up."

• Lopakhin: "Lord, thou gavest us immense forests, unbounded fields and the widest horizons, and living in the midst of them, we should indeed be giants—"

• Marchbanks: "I no longer desire happiness. Life is nobler than that."

• Hamlet: "The rest is silence."

Before the Words

Pay particular attention to the myriad sensory responses that precede and supersede the words that a person is speaking. Especially in moments of self-revelation or clarity about his destiny, pay attention to what the person is listening to, where his eyes are looking, what his fingers are touching. Learn to perceive how the words we speak are only a tiny part of the small vocal part of our total response at any one moment.

Discover how important sensory response is to the totality of response that lines of dialogue represent for dramatic characters. Create the stimuli and the responses that lead up to the utterance of a line (sometimes a lifetime of significant responses, sometimes simply the five minutes of responses leading immediately to the line).

You need not create a complete character to work on this, nor concern yourself with dramatic interplay and the scene. Simply use the character traits and the responses that you already have stored up. Keep the focus on your capacity to respond to all the significant stimuli that launch a character into a scene or lead a character to one of those surface-bursting significant lines.

- Lopakhin: "I bought the orchard!"

Create the auction. What does Lopakhin wear? Why? What is Gaev wearing? What are his hands doing? Where are his eyes looking? Does Lopakhin notice? Why or why not? What size is the room? Where are Lopakhin and Gaev in relation to everyone else, or in relation to the auctioneer? Who bids against Lopakhin right up to the end? (Is it another former peasant? Why or why not? What's the play about?) Create stimuli and respond to them right up to and including the moment when the auctioneer bangs down the gavel and says, "Sold to Yermolay Lopakhin, the merchant."

During the carriage ride home from the train station, when does Gaev decide to buy fish? Why does he need to? Given his sensitive sense of smell, why herring? Create the sound of horse's hooves on cobblestone streets, then along the dirt road out of town. Night sounds and smells. Be specific. Is there talking between the two on the ride? Perhaps there's a loose spring in Lopakhin's seat. Does the carriage belong to him now?

At the eastate, Lopakhin walks up the path to the house he bought only hours ago. What does he see? Standing against the sky, see the veranda and the carved wooden columns. See the carved frame of the door: Is it polished? (Why or why not?) Perhaps he could save it to put on the administration building for the housing development he plans here. Has he ever turned the brass knob on the door and walked in before? In the foyer where he usually stands and waits, hat in hand, is the smell of old polish on wood. Since Lubov's return, does her perfume linger in the air? Perhaps he starts to take his hat off, then, "Hell, this is my house now." Is there a chuckle, or a pang of remorse, or both?

Gaev instinctively leads the way up the stairs. Are there tears in his eyes? Does Lopakhin see Gaev's shoulders more stooped than usual? As Lopakhin's hands touch the bannister, they thrill to "this is my bannister." Upstairs in the ballroom, not just music, but that little Jewish orchestra playing, perhaps, "Over the Waves"? How well? Can Lopakhin tell?

Lopakhin sees Lubov. What color is her dress? She's done her hair in a new way for the party. What's his response? Part of him relives the crying needful peasant boy with the bloody nose every time he's in Lubov's presence. And so he goes on right up to, "I bought the orchard."

Why does he knock over the table?

• Nina: "Am I late?"

What has she been doing for the hour previous to her entrance? Create the situation and the environment with all the senses responding to specific stimuli: The rising moon, the ride around the lake. Can she smell it? The wind whips through her hair. When does she get off the horse? What happens to her just before she plunges into the clearing? What does she see?

• Romeo: "But soft, what light through yonder window breaks?"

Begin outside the orchard walls. Create the hot humid Verona night, the stars (Is his lucky constellation visible?), the distant sound of Mercutio and Benvolio calling to him. Create the force that finally pulls him over the orchard wall and back to the Capulet house. Create the sounds and smells of a night garden. Be specific. See the silhouette of the house looming against the night sky. Somewhere a twig snaps. A Capulet guard!? Does he have his rapier with him? And then—light!

• Treplev: "I was so low as to shoot this sea gull."

What has he been doing since the end of Act I? Create imaginatively, to select responses that lead him directly to Act II. How does he come to take a rifle with him today? Why does he shoot a sea gull? Improvise and discover.

• Juliet: "The clock struck nine when I did send the nurse...."

What has she been doing since nine o'clock in the morning? Why does she come into the courtyard? Create the noonday sun, the light and the shadows. Smell the roses that climb the trellises. Which gate will the nurse be most likely to come through on her way back from town? Is there a sundial in the courtyard, or a carving of cupid, or a bench? Create them through Juliet's responses. Lead her directly to this first line.

- Macbeth: "If it were done when 'tis done 'twere well it were done quickly."

Create the banquet. Have you ever visited a Scottish castle, or seen photos? What does the banquet hall look like? What kind of tables and chairs are there? Where does light come from?

Create the drinking, the toasts, the music, the shouting of oaths. Create Duncan in the seat of honor, lifting a goblet in a toast to Macbeth, "The finest soldier and the bravest, most loyal subject a king could have." Create Lady Macbeth at his side. Create the stimuli that relentlessly, inevitably, finally lead Macbeth to push his chair away from the table before he realizes what he is doing. He stands. A quick glance at Lady Macbeth's face, momentarily gone pale. A mumbled excuse. Then, away. Why does he need to leave the room? Why does he come out here? Get him to the point at which he must speak the words.

Continue in the same manner with these lines:

- Candida: "Come here dear and let me look at you."

- Hamlet: "O, that this too too sullied flesh would...."

- Hedda: "You have no idea, Judge, how mortally bored I have been."

- Medvedenko: "Why do you always wear black?"

- Lady Macbeth: "My hands are of your color though I shame to wear a heart so white."

- Viola: "The lady of the house, which is she?"

- Orsino: "If music be the food of love, play on."

- Mercutio: "O then I see Queen Mab hath been with you...."

- Arkadina: "I'm an actress not a banker."

Create all the sensory responses that lead up to the saying of the line. If the line is the beginning of a scene (Nina's first entrance line), then proceed straightforwardly: Nina at home, trying to get out of the house, watching for the rising moon (Let the play tell you which stimuli are significant), hoping her mother and stepfather will not see that she is sneaking out, riding around the lake, jumping down off the horse to run through the woods.

Others are more deep-rooted: Hedda's line goes back at least to last year's party when she agreed to let Tesman walk her home. Suddenly, in the company of the judge, a man who may be able to understand, because of an appropriate opening in their conversation, because her hand touches the back of the sofa and her eyes see the vulgar flowered pattern in the carpet and the heavy green velvet curtains over the windows, suddenly, the truth bursts forth into language.

What is the Judge's response? Why? What does he see and hear specifically and sense kinesthetically as he and Hedda chat?

What series of responses leads Medvedenko to ask the straightforward question, "Why do you always wear black?" Note: Avoid creating a series of generalized philosophical or psychological abstractions inside his head that lead to the line; rather it is a series of direct, literal responses to specific sensory details. Let the play lead you as you set up all the stimuli. For each line, provide direct stimuli to each of your senses, including the kinesthetic.

After you work on these, take each and write it out as though it were a sequence in a novel as discussed in Chapter 3.

Exits and Entrances

Observe people making entrances and exits in everyday life. What do those responses reveal about them individually? How, through specific response, do they reveal where they have just come from? What do they do upon entering the environment? What does this reveal about them and about their relationship to this place? How do they influence the rhythms and tempos of the environment they enter? How do they affect the forward flow of the situation they entered? Why?

Observe exits. Observe the play among the various forces at work on the person who is exiting: How strong is the pull to leave?

How is it revealed? How strong is the opposing force to stay? Connected to what specific stimuli? Account for the loss (or not) of a quality of energy or vitality when a person exits. Note the adjustments made by the people left in the situation to account for the loss of one of the contributing members.

The words "entrance" and "exit" are playwrighting terms. No character ever simply "enters" or "exits." Characters are human beings coming from a specific place, having left it for a specific reason. They are coming to the stage place for a specific reason which will determine "how" they enter and what they are doing as they enter. They have an objective, something they want to accomplish as they come here. They are responding to details of the environment. They see or hear something specific; perhaps they sense something kinesthetically, and they respond. Their objective may be challenged, supported, altered, weakened or distorted by what happens to them until something happens that makes them finally leave. They flee, they are ejected, they slink away, they rush off to somewhere more important; but they take their life, their needs, their conflict, and their future objectives with them. Consequently, they sustain our suspenseful interest in them till the next time they appear. It is the job of the characters who take over the stage action to top the exit and maintain the tension between the world offstage and the world on stage.

• Improvise Marchbanks' entrance: Note Shaw's description. Refer to the novel exercise in Chapter Three and the actor's capacity to turn description into actual motivated behavior. Incorporate the behavior into motivated responses to specific sensory stimuli. Where is the opposition, or the comedy?

• Improvise a return home for Candida before Marchbanks even comes into their lives. What does Candida always do when she returns home after a few days away? Why?

• Describe the principle of opposites as it is at work here. Characters often enter the stage space in response to some specific stimulus in the environment immediately preceding the entrance, so that their body is being pulled in two directions as they enter. In Act II, for instace, Lubov looks back at a blueberry bush as she comes into the stage space, is arrested by the sight of the old chapel and the associations it touches off.

• Design and describe Arkadina's entrances in I and IV and her exits in I, II, III. Do them.

• What do you reveal about yourself when, as Hedda you make your Act I entrance?

• Examine Shakespeare's entrances and exits. Except for those few scenes when people are "discovered" in the inner-below area, all scenes begin with entrances and end with exits. Purely on the kinesthetic level, what are the implications of this construction for the meaning of Shakespeare?

• Note how long it takes for Lopakhin to actually exit in Act I following his vocal declaration to leave and his body's decision to go.

• Study Medvedenko's attempts at leaving the house in Act III of *The Sea Gull*. What do we know about him by the way other people respond to his exit?

The entire fourth acts of *Three Sisters* and *The Cherry Orchard* are groups making their last departure from a beloved home. Within the dynamics of that great climactic exit, notice the tributary force of the individual entrances and exits and reentrances. Nobody is better than Chekhov at dramatizing arrivals and departures.

• Look closely at the end of *The Cherry Orchard*. Everyone exits. The play must be over. The axes begin to fell the trees in the orchard. Slow fade? No. Here comes Fiers, the Forgotten One. And Chekhov the master playwright exploits, even subverts, the meaningful rhythms of theatre to create new kinesthetically experiential meaning.

3

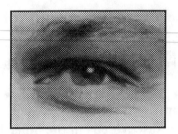

The
Imagination

*"My gift for imagination
was more important to me than all my talent for absorbing
scientific facts."*

— *Albert Einstein*

The Power to Create

The preceding two chapters deal with direct experience
human behavior through the senses, helping actors
become true perceivers and storehouses of revelato:
response. The goal is to use the world and their individual selves f
field study, and to develop a source of building materials for the cr
ative imagination. The organizing question behind the work on se
sory perception might be, "Why do people do what they do?"

This chapter focuses on the creative use of indirect and vicarious experience by which the actor's imagination builds from known elements to the unknown goal. We will explore the use of other art forms to help in the actor's creative tasks, and how to let various elements of a play stimulate the imagination. Any part of nature can serve as a stimulus to the imagination and actors must learn to use all the world around them as a source of creative stimulation. To the question "Why?" our work on the actor's imagination adds, "What if...?"

Imagination in Science

The genius of people like John Dalton, the English chemist, and Albert Einstein, the German physicist, lies in their capacity to ask innocent, even impertinent, questions which generate cataclysmic answers. Dalton asked himself concrete questions about the way elements combine by weight. Why, when water is composed of oxygen and hydrogen, do exactly the same amounts always make a given amount of water? Why, when carbon dioxide or methane are made, are there constancies of weight? Of the one transparent, searching question about the weights that determine the construction of simple molecules, Dalton's atomic theory was established.

The mythologized story of Einstein tells us that on his way to and from work each day his train went past a clock tower. One day he wondered, "What would happen to time if this train moved away from the clock tower at the speed of light? Why? What if?" Physics and our concept of reality changed forever. No matter if the story is apocryphal; as Alvina Krause once said to me, "If it's a lie, it's a true lie."

In an article titled "In Search of the Cure for AIDS" (Rolling Stone), Northwestern University Medical school HIV researcher Steve Wolinsky was quoted:

"How is it transmitted? Where does it go? I mean, we're really just trying to answer the questions that an eight-year-old might ask."

A few paragraphs later the article's author, Robert Sullivan, writes,

> "Among children born of HIV-infected mothers, an intriguing statistic presents itself: More than two-thirds are not infected with HIV. And the 8-year-old question is simply, Why?"

The suggestion is that profound answers come from learning to ask simple, even childlike questions.

In the Arts

Imagination is the creative power with which artists translate their particular experiences and communicate them to an audience. It is the conduit that writers use to convey their impressions of humanity to the reader through their love of words and story structure. Georgia O'Keefe wrote this about painting in a letter to Sherwood Anderson (September, 1923):

> I feel that a real living form is the natural result of the individual's effort to create the living thing out of the adventure of the spirit into the unknown—where it has experienced something—felt something—it has not understood—and from that experience comes the desire to make the unknown known—By known I mean the thing that means so much to the person that he wants to put it down—clarify something he feels but does not clearly understand—sometimes he partially knows why— sometimes he doesn't—sometimes it is all working in the dark—but a working that must be done—Making the unknown—known—in terms of one's medium is all absorbing—(The National Gallery of Art, Washington, Boston, 1987.)

In his search for the right sound for the spaceships in the *Star Wars* movies, Benjamin Burtt, who received an Academy Award for sound design, went to Air Force bases and military installations around the country to tape various airplane and rocket engines. He studied these for weeks but ultimately the sound that successfully sparked his imagination was the drone of an air conditioner in his hotel room.

Burtt was creating something for a fantasy world, but he went in search of stimuli in the real world. Logically, he explored sources that were analogous to what he wanted to create. Wonderfully, something he could not have considered directly applicable beforehand became the source of his creation.

When we ask, "What if we take this reality and apply it to fictional circumstances?" original creation happens.

For Actors

Writers must learn to use language, and painters learn to create with canvas, brushes and paint. Actors must learn to develop an imaging power that creates instinctively, in behavioral terms, human responses to specific stimuli. Imagination is the power by which actors work from life to create the theatrical realities suggested by the play. This is not simply, nor even primarily, an intellectual or mental process since, as the preceding chapter illustrated, actors "think" creatively in terms of actual human behavior. They create in their totality, with physical images and real experiences which they have stored up in their literal self, not in some intangible or spiritual space thought of as "the imagination." The actor's creative imagination is the power by which known realities (or "one's medium" to use another of O'Keefe's phrases), are transformed into the unknown reality, namely, the characters, relationships, circumstances and themes of the play.

Before they become self-conscious, children's imaginations are instinctively "actorly": They go immediately into direct, illustrative action. Children exemplify Stanislavski's "magic If," creating realities purely in terms of behavior. Anyone who has watched children at play knows that they never seem stymied by how they should do something. They go directly into action that is a specific response to significant stimuli, turning a chair and a carpet into a castle, or creating universes out of a hill of sand, or making a time machine from a pile of abandoned junk.

I remember watching two children playing in the courtyard of my apartment building. There is a walkway to a fountain in the center, high stone walls and the semblance of sculptured gardens. The children discovered a frog in the fountain, and suddenly: "You be the evil Queen and he's a prince you turned into a frog." As the little girl said, "I'll be the princess," she pulled up her spine, her arms went out like a ballerina's, creating the long sleeves of her imaginary medieval gown. She lifted her head to balance a medieval cone hat, or a tiara. She stood on tiptoe and gazed regally down the courtyard path to her castle. Her imagination instantly translated the idea "princess" into action and motivated behavior. (What this particular example might reveal about socialized gender role behavior is another topic.) She didn't just make up this behavior from thin air; these were stored response images instantly creating an active, responsive embodiment of the idea "princess." She had perceived and retained the behavior from life, and from the pictures and descriptions in books, films and cartoons. Actors can learn from children how to accumulate an entire world as a source of imaginative creativity as well as how to let those images play easily in truthful interaction.

Why? What If?

The imagination works through reality. First, just let the imagination play actively with stimuli.

Choose an object that has significance for you. Simply respond to it, let it play on your senses and stimulate your imagination. Let the following descriptions clarify what you feel, but never let intellect become a substitute for actual sensory experience:

• Eva picks up a trophy she won in a high school swim meet. She puts herself back in the sports complex the day she won the trophy. Instantly the walls of the classroom disappear as Eva responds to the vastness of the aquatic center, the rows of spectators, the vaulting ceiling. Her chest rises in pride, she lifts her arms to acknowledge the applause of the spectators. She smiles, turns, walks, and sets the trophy on a stand back in her own bedroom.

• Joel hangs wind chimes and becomes a little boy in his grandmother's garden. He looks and his eyes go wide in wonder as a butterfly floats by. The little boy reaches up and touches the chimes. He begins to smile, his spine lifts and his arms extend as if he were flying.

For now, there are no real expectations; simply let yourself respond, as other stimuli suggest themselves beyond the object. Ask questions and let answers happen easily: What else in the room belongs with your object? Why? What qualities in you, in terms of actual behavior, do these things animate or manifest? If there were a play about you, why would the playwright want to include this object in the environment?

Let your imagination play with opposing elements of the environment, and in yourself as they are manifested by these externals:

- The swimming trophy as opposed to the score of *Sunday in the Park with George*

- The windchimes opposite the package of condoms in your pocket

- The perfectly ordered desk opposite the overflowing laundry bag

- Treplev's daisy as opposed to the rifle he uses to shoot the sea gull

- Which parts of the "home"-you are brought to your school environment? Which are suppressed? Why?

Let yourself respond to any number of interesting objects even if you have no life-experience association with them. Simply allow your actor's imagination set your responsive totality galloping:

- Pick up a candlestick. Heft it, look at it, respond to it, light the candle. Let these responses to the candle stimulate your imagination. What do these activities suggest to you? There is no right thing to do. Simply let your imagination begin to create specific stimuli for your senses to respond to.

- Kyle turns a table in the classroom into an altar by placing the candlestick on it and the room becomes a church, Kyle an altar boy or someone praying alone.

- Donna lifts the candle and turns the rehearsal room into an old house with dark stairways and forbidden passages; the bank of old lighting instruments in the corner becomes a wine cellar filled with vintage bottles. The imagination lets it happen and the person responds truthfully to the stimuli; there is no need to decide beforehand.

As one actor begins to respond, another may prompt by asking questions: "Is there a window in this room?" If the first actor turns and sees a window, the second may continue, "Better peek through the curtains." And then, "What do you see?" taking cues from the first actor's responses.

• Turn that tiny metal rehearsal table into a long carved oak table by simply putting the candlestick on it and responding as if it were. Analyze that "as if it were." Some actors have the ability to walk into a room and suddenly it's a church, or a corporate office, or a forest glen. What do they do? Essentially, they have the ability to put the specifics "out there." It's not "in their mind's eye"; rather, they see and hear specific details. Their muscles sense the size of the room, the feel of the space, and they nonconsciously respond. In effect, they turn the room into a church by trusting their senses to respond to the stimuli that create a church. They have already stored up responses which can easily be activated when their actor selves need them.

• Turn the stage floor into flagstones strewn with straw. Turn that pewter cup into an Elizabethan drinking mug, and lift it high in a toast. Let the wall in front of you become the stone wall of a castle hung with a gold, red and purple tapestry: Simply see and respond to the pattern as a child could. Are there *fleur-de-lis*, or unicorns? Is there metallic thread? Bang the mug down on the long wooden table. A shout goes up from the people around you; arms draped in red velvet sleeves and gold embroidery glitter in the candlelight. Hands punch the air raising the cups in a toast.

The candlestick becomes one of twenty standing on the table; torches on the walls sputter their golden light. A group of musicians play madrigals in the corner of the room, and at the head of the table Capulet stands and puts his arm around Tybalt. (What specific visual details do you respond to that say "Capulet"? Let the play help.) A servant bears a platter with a roast pig on it, followed by two more with great pitchers of wine; boisterous young men wearing masks bound down the staircase. You are in the Capulet house for the ball as Romeo sees Juliet in torchlight and the course of lives is changed.

What object might you choose in order to create these:

• Hedda in her parlour?

• Macbeth in the anteroom waiting for the sound of Lady Macbeth's bell?

• Lopakhin at the auction?

Work on these situations without pressure "to succeed" or "to do them right." Simply explore. Discover objects that will suggest significant stimuli and let yourself respond.

The Dream

The students at Theatre Arts U. close their eyes and "go to sleep." Their imaginations respond freely to stimuli because in dreams they are not constrained by the logic of everyday reality. The teacher provides a sensory stimulus: Perhaps the slow dripping of water into a large vessel, or the sound of a dinner bell. Perhaps the scent of lilacs, or the feel of velvet touching their cheeks. One of the students is prompted to let her imagination move her into action, to live out her "dream" in actual behavior. The teacher carefully and unobtrusively prompts with questions and suggestions, stimulating the student's imagination for further response within this context.

The teacher passes a bouquet of fresh lilies-of-the-valley past the students' noses. Joel immediately smiles and sighs. "Where are you?" the teacher asks.

"At my grandmother's," he says, "at the side of the house." Again he smiles. "There are lilies-of-the-valley there. It's my favorite spot."

"Stand up," the teacher says quietly. Joel rises.

"Open your eyes. See the lilies-of-the-valley." He does. He moves toward them. "Are you allowed to pick them?"

"No," he says with the look of a little boy who is aware of the rules.

"Do you want to?"

"Yes," and a glimmer of mischief passes into his eyes.

"Is anyone watching?"

They re-create a childhood adventure; or perhaps they move into fantasy: "Hear a bee buzzing. Do you like bees?" If Joel says "Yes," the teacher may respond with a description of a swarm of friendly giant bees as they take him on a honey-making adventure. If he says, "No," they can go off on a scary story in which a swarm of killer bees surround, the house and threatens the whole town.

Anything is possible if the participants respond truthfully to specific sensory stimuli.

The same principle applies to drama:

• Go to sleep, and become Hedda. You need not be all that Hedda must be, simply be as much of her as you can be, without anxiety or self-consciousness. Let yourself respond. You may discover something new about her, or you may verify character traits that you have already incorporated into your being.

• Hear the sound of people whispering, gossiping; smell the overpowering odor of bouquets of flowers (When was the last time Hedda was in a room with so many flowers?) Let yourself respond and discover. There are clues in the play to the kind of dream that will reveal Hedda, but each person's "dream" will be different. There really is no "right" dream to have, though there will be varying degrees of appropriateness. Your goal is to come to a fuller understanding of Hedda. The teacher may prompt and ask questions that incorporate significant elements from the play, trying to clarify the deepest motivating force of the character in terms of active responses.

Joy, because of her own upbringing, had a difficult time understanding Hedda's trapped sense and her fear of scandal. She began her dream exploration by walking through a room filled with roses, honeysuckle and lilies. I suggested that the odor intensify, that the flowers multiply, even begin to enlarge. Other students stood up and became flowers closing in, towering over Hedda. As they moved toward her, she cringed. I pointed out a door which she walked toward, but as the flowers closed in I said, "The door is receding!" She panicked and made to run. "Don't let anyone know you're frightened!" I commanded. As she tried to repress the panic, the flowers began to giggle and point at her. I clapped my hand over her mouth, ordering her: "Call out! Shout! Maybe someone can save you." She turned toward the class members who laughed at her as she struggled to break free of me and to escape the room. I held tighter. "Here's a pistol," I said, putting one in her hand, "Do something!" She wheeled around and pointed it at me.

"You are at a reception for Tesman," I called out and the students immediately became party guests. I smiled at our Hedda and said, "You must be Mrs. Tesman, are you not? I am Ambassador

Solvang, here to present your husband with a research award." Her heart beating, her spine tense, wildness in her eyes, her breath coming in labored gasps, a pistol in her hand, she was forced to smile, to pretend to relax, to extend a hand and to introduce herself. With effort, her voice came measured, pleasant, "So lovely to meet you." Playing beneath, barely perceptible, was a trapped human being, being stifled, but determined not to let anyone see.

Joy said, "Oh, I see! I used to have this same response when we'd go to visit my Aunt Meredith. I hated the smell of her house and she always made tea that was cold and had too much milk in it. But you had to smile and drink it and thank her. Sometimes I wanted to scream, but I couldn't." She then re-created the experience for the class, which revealed the motivated behavior of Hedda Gabler. Dream exploration helped Joy to connect to an experience that touched off with understanding the Hedda within her. We immediately asked Joy to be Hedda standing in the doorway to the parlor, looking at the sunlight streaming in patches on the patterned flowered carpet. Tesman comes scampering up with a glass of warm milk in his hand. "Would you like some?" he asks.

• For Juliet's nurse, use the smells of food and drink as the stimuli to touch off dream logic responses. The aim is to get her responding to the stimuli of personal comfort where she will find what is most important to the nurse.

• How would you start someone off on a Lopakhin dream?

• What stimulus might lead to discovery as Oswald dreams?

Be sure to actually see, smell, and hear stimuli. Questions should not be asked in a removed, intellectual manner that prompts actors to think of reasoned answers. The questioner's voice should be a manifestation of the stimulus being provided or the question being asked. The actor's answers should not be analytical or objective, but always the vocal part of the total response experience. They should never be a substitute for response or a prompt to make the body do what the mind decided. The voice becomes part of the in-dream responses.

ELEMENTS FROM DRAMA AND LIFE

• See that clock on the mantel? Does it belong in this room? Does it belong on a Chekhov mantle or an Ibsen table? Why or why not?

• What does an Ibsen stove do to an Ibsen room? Why? Where might you find stimuli for your imagination to create the Tesman parlor, or Lubov's nursery?

• What kind of fireplace and mantle does the Reverend Morell have in his study? Perceive and store up responses to a Victorian library and fireplace. To find clues, go to a restored Victorian house or to a museum. Find books that deal with the subject through photographs, drawings, and detailed descriptions.

Turn the room you are working in into the room you see in the photograph; become a Victorian person at home in such a room and let yourself respond. Take a piece of wood from the hod and put it on the fire. Pick up the poker and adjust the logs. Turn to look at the desk on the wall opposite. See James sitting there hunched over his Bible. Is there enough light coming from his lamp? Then go into action as Candida.

Learn to turn everything into stimuli for your creative imagination. The world is the source for your imagination. And the imagination becomes creative only if the realistic sensory response to a stimulus is vivid enough to enlarge of its own accord.

For example:

• You go to the lake. As you stand on the rock you actually see the color, the form, the movement of the water. See a gull flying over the lake; muscles perceive the movement, the dip, the soaring. Hear the tempo of the waves, feel the spray.

• Let yourself intensify the responses until the water darkens and the roar grows loud and the gulls cry out. The spray slaps your face and the clouds darken as they rush across the sky. The lake enlarges to become the North Sea; you are Hamlet standing on a parapet watching the seventh wave come in. Your muscles swell with the progress of the wave; it breaks and you hear yourself saying to the rhythm of the breaking waves, "To be or not to be, that is the question...."

Until and unless they are touched off by images and rooted in reality, "To be" will only be words.

• "Dear, honored bookcase! I salute your existence." What must the actor creating Gaev see, touch, perceive? What must the actor do to turn a rehearsal table into a Russian bookcase with glass doors, little polished brass handles, shelves of leatherbound volumes of Pushkin, drawers containing mama's favorite stationery still inside?

• Turn a rehearsal space into Hedda's parlour through sense response. Begin with your own reality.

In *A Challenge for the Actor*, Uta Hagen describes her concept of "historical imagination" this way:

> When we tap the available sources in literature, historical biographies, paintings, sculpture, music, pottery and artifacts, and those we contact as tourists, we must experience everything personally, imaginatively identifying with it, putting ourselves into it as though we were walking on those floors, drinking from that goblet, climbing into the canopied bed in that ruffled nightshirt, extinguishing the taper on the little table at the bedside, listening to the horses clopping on the cobblestones below our window—whether we are reading about it in a novel or biography, looking at it in a painting, or traveling through a historic house in Boston or in Europe. Our job is to make ourselves participants in other worlds until we can see, hear, touch, taste, and smell them. (p.216)

• Perhaps you love photography or dance. Perhaps you enjoy going out into the countryside to sketch. Encourage creativity from the point of view of your strengths. In the first chapter I suggested you draw lines on a page to stimulate improvising relationships among characters. Try going around your house taking imaginary photos of your family that will best illustrate truths about them. Or draw a cartoon of Marchbanks greeting Burgess.

Then try these examples:

• Give Hamlet a camera and let him photograph illustrative interactions in Elsinore. What do you discover about Hamlet, Elsinore, and the play?

• Let Juliet create a dance to describe her relationship with her mother and father. Have Lady Capulet do the same.

• Lovborg sketches Hedda and Tesman. Then Tesman describes Hedda to a portrait artist. Judge Brack describes the painting of Hedda he imagines hanging above the mantlepiece.

• What might Marchbanks do to capture his responses to the Morell household?

Test yourself:

• Somebody tosses an interesting object, perhaps a large medallion on a chain, to Eva and calls out, "Arkadina." Eva catches the medallion and instantaneously turns it into a mirror to check her appearance. Without time to "think," she becomes Arkadina. (Eva might also let the medallion become a broach to wear for an autograph party or something else equally appropriate.) When Arkadina is satisfied with what she sees in the mirror she goes out to greet her public, tosses the medallion to Jerry and calls out, "Polonius."

• Jerry puts the medallion around his neck, holds on to his "badge of office" and goes down the hall in search of a problem to solve, tossing the medallion to Donna and calling out "Laura Wingfield."

• Donna immediately turns the medallion into a stand for her latest crystal animal.

This is a terrific exercise to test whether or not you can instantly elicit significant responses in a character without worrying about what you don't know. You might be pleasantly surprised to discover how much you already know in muscles, nerves, and sensory response, about a great many dramatic characters.

Play Titles

Your imagination works to discover the playwright's created drama. Learn to allow the playwright to stimulate your imagination. Play with titles, remembering that for the actor, imagination must mean action, response, behavior. Why is it *Hedda Gabler*, not *Hedda Tesman?* Of "Gabler" and "Tesman" which is the more socially resonant name to the Norwegian ear? What is the implication for the actor? Let your Hedda do what "Hedda Gabler" means in realistic behavior terms. Then do what "Hedda Tesman" implies.

Research what the Norwegian word that we translate as *Ghosts* refers to in Norwegian myth, as well as in everyday reality. Let your imagination play with that word as you explore the drama.

Think of *A Midsummer-Night's Dream*. According to legend, what traditionally happens during the mid-summer night? Do schools still have a Sadie Hawkins dance? Illustrate with interaction: Boys on one side, girls on the other. At the stroke of midnight, girls go off in chase to find a man. What is the logic of a dream? Anything can happen. Whooosh, Martha, you're in love with Kyle. Throw your arms around him. Whooosh, you hate him; turn around, fall in love with the first person you see. It's Eva! Kyle, you fall in love with Eva, too. Whooosh! Joy's eyes are beautiful.

Work this way until everyone is motivated by the comedic joy of sexual jealousy and instantaneous dream logic that motivates *A Midsummer-Night's Dream*. What is the play dramatizing about "Lord, what fools these mortals be!" in matters of love and sex?

Notice that the behavioral theme of *A Midsummer-Night's Dream* motivates the action of *Miss Julie* and *A Little Night Music*, even *Othello*. What clues stimulate your imagination to create the tempos and overall tone of each play? Be specific. What are the communication goals of each?

Why is it called *The Sea Gull?* Is it only Nina to whom the title refers? The destruction of the sea gull need not be literal death: Sorin is an old man in whom the sea gull responses died years ago. Medvedenko is a young man who seems to have had his sea gull-ness squelched from the very beginning. Trigorin carries a notebook and a pencil to endlessly scratch down words that will become a perfect, simple, stereotyped description and he thinks he's captured it. He whittles his own fishing poles and takes more delight in them than in his pencil and notebook. (Notice that when they are leaving in Act III, he tells Yakov to save the fishing poles and get rid of the books.) Try a free-association "dream ballet" in which Trigorin becomes the sea gull he once wanted to be; in which Treplev becomes the sea gull he so desperately hopes to become. What is destroyed in the play when a sea gull is shot and stuffed?

Characters' Names

Begin simply with the medieval play *Everyman*. Embody the name "Friendship." What elemental things does Friendship do that are the expression of what motivates Friendship? The question is asked in terms of actual, doable behavior, not abstract qualities. Improvise until your spine is motivated by this simple, direct behavior. Try incorporating the old phrase, "Wine, women, and song" into the play's concept of friendship.

Embody in direct action "Good Deeds." What are "good deeds" motivated to do in literal, active terms? Perhaps a contemporary equivalent in Red Cross relief efforts, or Mother Teresa, can stimulate your imagination. What do you do when you do Good Deeds?

What does the title *The School for Scandal* stimulate your action imagination to do? What motivates a school? Set yourself into speculative action. Now add the motivated behavior that the word "scandal" suggests to you. Is there an opposite here? Irony? Does it touch off your comic sense?

Let yourself literally do "Backbite" or "Sneerwell" until your spine, your eyes, your feet, your muscles, are truly motivated to do what the names imply. Learn to read a play for all of its clues. I saw a production of the play in which the servant, whose name is Trip, played a perfectly efficient British retainer, always where he needed to be. How could he and his director have missed the implication in his name? Of course, a playwright sometimes deliberately plays on the irony of a character's name exhibiting directly opposite behavior: What do you suppose Oscar Wilde had in mind for the butler Merriman in *The Importance of Being Earnest?*

Benvolio comes from Latin words that mean "I want good" or "I wish you well." Let your spine become motivated by "I wish you well." Really do it until you are effortlessly motivated to wish people well. Although everyone who does this will do something individual, all who truly are motivated by "I wish you well" will have an uplifted and outgoing spine; eyes searching, looking for the needs of others. What does his voice do? What other kinds of behavior automatically happen when you are motivated to wish others well? Does this suggest something to you about the way Benvolio handles Mercutio, Lord Montague, Tybalt? Incorporate the opposing clues that are suggested by Mercutio's description of Benvolio when he gets his anger up (III, i).

Discover opposites among characters: Benvolio (do it) comes up against Mercutio (Do it. What does mercury do? Why?) who comes up against Tybalt, "The Prince of Cats" (Do it. What motivates a cat? How is it manifested in spine, walk, shoulders, eyes). Sense implicit drama in the active, behavioral oppositions suggested by the names as three actors motivated as these three beings interact with one another.

Play with the following examples. What clues to character and behavior do the names suggest in terms of behavior? Are there ironies and oppositions in character?

• Marchbanks (what would the name "Maybanks" suggest?)

• Candida (Add "candid" to the description Shaw provides upon her first entrance. I have a friend who has a low opinion of Shaw; she likes to imagine that he knew that "candida" means "a vaginal yeast infection.")

• Proserpine (the Goddess of the Spring. Play with this image. What behavior does it suggest to you?) Now let it be "Prossy." Prossy Garnett, a secretary who has shut down all response. What happens when she has a bit too much champagne before Act III?

• What does "Lubov" mean in Russian?

Musical Comedy Songs

Musical comedy songs, (the melody, the rhythm, the harmony) are character motivation in themselves. Let the music animate you, let your spine and your muscles become the kinesthetic embodiment of the music. Listen and respond to the various lines of the music (melody, harmony, bass line), not only to the words. Let the melody play on the surface, but let counterpoint and other rhythmic lines play deeper inside. Find the spine of the character in each of these songs:

• "Rose's Turn" (*Gypsy*)

• "Reviewing the Situation" (*Oliver!*)

• "Send in the Clowns" (*A Little Night Music*)

• "Don't Rain on My Parade" (*Funny Girl*)

- "My Boy Bill" (*Carousel*)

- "With a Little Bit o' Luck" (*My Fair Lady*)

Look as well for opposite songs sung by the same character: "My Man" and "Don't Rain on My Parade" from *Funny Girl* as two opposites in Fanny Brice, or Nancy's "As Long as He Needs Me" and "Oompah-pah" from *Oliver!*

Character Tune

Do you often find yourself humming the same nameless tune as you walk along? Do you suddenly break into song? Is it habitually the same kind of song? People can be thought of as having a little tune or melody playing through them that can be expressed in the rhythm of their walk, even their thought patterns. What's yours? How does it manifest itself in you? Be specific and literal. Is there an opposite tune that plays through you just as well? What parts of you does it tend to activate most?

- Let your father's tune play through you. What happens to you when you let it happen to you? How does it help you to understand him? Create a characterization of him by letting his tune become his motivated spine.

- Discover the inner tune of the President of the United States.

- Study your local librarian and discover the inner tune.

- Try Dr. Dorn and his melody. What is its opposite?

- Prossy has a little tune playing inside her that is an opposite to the efficient, tight, closed-off secretary who operates through her external layers. Marchbanks touches that inner person in Act II and a little champagne in Act III brings it out too.

- Discover the Friar Laurence melody. The rhythms of his language and the singsong end-rhymes of his lines are clues.

- What is Hedda's inner tune? Played on what kind of instrument? Let it play through you until it is playing you, until your imagination has let it take over. Then put on the Hedda smile and let her greet Judge Brack and Aunt Julie. Let the external melody that others hear play on top of the driving inner tune.

- Explore singing voices: Of Morell, Candida and Marchbanks, who is the baritone, the tenor, the contralto? Where does Burgess fit in? Prossy is a soprano who has squeezed all beauty from her voice. A little champagne before Act III, and what happens?

Take a cue from Prokofiev's *Peter and the Wolf*:

• What sound suggests your roommate to you?

• Your best friend is a melody or a musical instrument. What does it do? Why?

• Do the same with Lopakhin, Judge Brack, Lady Capulet.

• Create the Nurse and Juliet as individual solos and then as a duet. What do you discover?

• Student Eva tells of her music teacher once saying to her, "You must learn to hear the unwritten melody in Mozart." Apply this idea to characterization, to acting, to drama.

The Living Poster

Posters free you from linear realistic logic but since they function almost on the plane of symbol or metaphor, they can test how deeply you understand essential character motivation, relationships and situations at the heart of the drama. Several people get together to create two or three "living posters" to advertise a play. Let them describe what they are doing, and why, as they arrange one another in a way that embodies the play's meaning. The very avenue of attack that "living poster" represents can lead you to discoveries you hadn't previously articulated. Remember, you can play non-human elements too.

Cartooning

Political cartoonists, with their strong points of view, clarify something essentially true about the situation they depict. In terms of character motivation and the ironies involved, they create a trenchant form of communication.

Try doing the same for plays:

• Draw a cartoon of the Nurse/Juliet relationship first from Juliet's point of view, then the Nurse's, and finally from the playwright's point of view. Then, embody these qualities in your own creations of the Nurse/Juliet relationship.

• Draw Hamlet at the moment he realizes that Ophelia isn't alone in the room for the nunnery scene.

• Draw a cartoon of Macbeth the soldier. Then Macbeth after Duncan's murder.

• Draw a cartoon that focuses on the relationship between Macbeth and Lady Macbeth

> 1.) Before the play starts
> 2.) During their encounter outside Duncan's banquet
> 3.) During the gathering when Banquo's ghost appears.

Painting

• Study nineteenth-century portraiture. The portraits by the Russian painter Repin offer valuable insights into the people of Chekhov's time.

• Study Leonardo, Caravaggio, El Greco. Their understanding of motivated spine, of characteristic hands and facial features, of opposition, of implicit gesture, as well as relationships within a group, can set off your own "thinking body" imagination to understand and create.

• Study the Impressionists. Let yourself become people in their paintings:

> 1.) If I were this person at this Renoir cafe....
> 2.) If I were this Monet barmaid.....
> 3.) If I were this woman in this Manet garden....

Let yourself respond and discover. Avoid inventing complex biographies and interactions, stories and plots. Simply let yourself respond to the stimuli and discover.

• How do the paintings of Munch help in creating the characters in Ibsen?

• Why do the illustrations of Aubrey Beardsley help create the people of Oscar Wilde?

• Is there a portrait from the nineteenth Century that can help suggest Hedda Gabler?

• Paint the beginning of Act II of *The Sea Gull.*

Photography

Photographs can serve much the same purpose as paintings. *Victorian Photographs*, by Bevis Hillier (David R. Godine, Publisher, 1976) and similar books offer terrific studies for plays set in the nineteenth century. (This particular volume contains a photo of Lady Churchill who is a dead ringer for Mrs. Saunders from Caryl Churchill's *Cloud 9*). There is also a Harry Baggley among the photographs.

Photographs for the Tsar (Robert Allshouse, ed., The Dial Press, 1980) can put you directly into situations with characters that Turgenev and Chekhov dramatize.

Old photos and post cards in second-hand stores are a treasure of stimuli to help you understand and create.

The reference room of the library will put you in touch with sources which stimulate your imagination and set it galloping in the right direction.

Other Suggestions

• Design a fabric print that evokes Macbeth.

• Become the newspaper reporter who interviews Tesman and Judge Brack after Hedda's death.

• Take a photo of Candida and Marchbanks before the fireplace.

• Paint the three sisters standing in the garden at the end of the play.

• Provide further examples.

Metaphor

"Metaphor" comes from the Greek "metapherein," (meta—over; pherein—to carry). It means "to transfer to one word the sense of another" and is defined as "a figure of speech in which one thing is likened to another different thing by being spoken of as if it were that other; implied comparison, in which a word or phrase ordinarily and primarily used of one thing is applied to another." "In his passion he was a raging bull" is an example of metaphor. "Metaphor" is different from "simile" in which one thing is likened to another with the word "like": "My love is like a red red rose." For the purposes of this book, however, I shall use the word "metaphor" to mean any kind of likening or analogizing.

We are used to metaphor as a literary device in everything from Homer's "rosy-fingered dawn" and "wine-dark sea," to this from a supermarket romance novel: "...his eyes, blue flames burning into hers with a searing impact..."

Metaphor, a form of artistic shorthand, is one way among many through which the artist seeks to make known the unknown, by working, as with any other aspect of the imagination, with and through known experience. You cannot imagine something that is not based in images you have already perceived, nor can you imagine something whose elements you have not perceived.

Popular fantasy art illustrates the idea of building to the unknown through the known. No matter how strange the planet, how unterrestrial the creatures, they are always fashioned from everyday perceivable earth realities. For example, the appearance and behavior of the creatures in the *Alien* movies, however alien they may be, derive in part from aspects of insect life, which become terrifying when enlarged to human scale. To a metamorphasic life process, which includes a human host immobilized in webbing to feed newly-hatched larvae, add dripping slimy "saliva"; a shiny black exoskeleton of durable silicone and, as part of the mouth, an inner cylinder of metallic teeth that protrudes like a mutilating machine; the speed of a mantis; greenish blood that can eat its way through anything like a super-acid; and you will have a creature the audience can believe in and be terrified by. However unique and otherworldly the entire creature, each of its separate elements is a perfectly recognizable earthly reality.

In the beautiful communicating power of metaphor, animated cartoons offer many brilliant examples.

From the Chicago Tribune of Sunday, November 24, 1991:

> Animation of the Beast [Walt Disney's *Beauty and the Beast*] was supervised by Glen Keane, who....began by looking at National Geographic animal studies, "lots of film of lions, baboons, bears and gorillas." The brow of the gorilla gave Keane an impression of strength of purpose, so he went over to the Los Angeles Zoo, got as close to the gorillas as he could, and drew studies. But it was in the American bison, or buffalo, that he found the sad, soulful gentleness he wanted to mix with the gorilla's strength.
>
> In his room at the studio, he hung a huge buffalo head on his wall for inspiration, gave the Beast a beard like a buffalo and began animating to the wide range of human emotions suggested by the recordings of Beast's voice, done by actor Robby Benson: anger, gruffness, tenderness and humor."

Even in animation, studying and perceiving real life are keys to true artistry. The flowers in Disney's *Alice in Wonderland* demonstrate motivated character behavior derived from metaphorical implications of shape and color. The purple iris lifts itself royally above Alice on its straight solid stem, bosom puffed out with a yellow lace jabot and a lorgnette of tendril from a nearby plant. The daffodils apparently take their cue from being "daffy dills" as they giggle and gurgle, their huge cylindrical noses and wreaths of petals flopping about.

In their book *Metaphors We Live By*, George Lakoff and Mark Johnson demonstrate that we depend on metaphor for communication much more than we actually realize. Indeed, it would be nearly impossible to carry on a conversation without using metaphor. (How does one "carry on" a conversation?) The book deals with the communicating power of metaphor through language, yet the authors make this illuminating statement:

In actuality we feel that no metaphor can ever be compre-
hended or even adequately represented independently of its
experiential basis.

It is at the primary level of experience, of course, that the actor takes
advantage of metaphor as a pathway toward understanding and communicating behavior. For the actor, metaphor exists in terms of
actual behavior, and stored-up experience with the metaphorizer is
critical for truthful creativity. A student once suggested that *Henry
IV's* Prince Hal was exactly like a particular kind of thoroughbred
pony with which he was familiar. I had never heard of the animal, so
my own responsive muscles and imaginative powers were stopped
dead; I stood immobile, unable to respond or to create. The creative force can only work with what it has experienced and stored up.
(What would be lacking in your understanding of Nina if you had
never heard of, read about, or seen a sea gull? And is the Russian
bird similar to the American one?)

By implication, it is the actor's responsibility to perceive and
store up as much of the world as is possible. The more you have
stored up with comprehension, the more you have to create with,
and the more readily you will grasp the significance of the elements
the playwright has included that will most clearly communicate the
play to an audience.

Working with Metaphor

"Herman waited in the darkness like a cobra, coiled and
ready to strike." The reader understands something about Herman
because the reader knows from first-hand or vicarious experience
what a cobra, coiled and ready to strike, is like. A reader who has no
experience of a cobra will know nothing more about Herman
because of the metaphor. If, however, the reader associates the word
"coiled" with a spring, then the process of metaphorizing helps the
reader to understand what this unknown "cobra" does. By extension,
the reader knows what is it about Herman he or she is being asked
to pay attention to.

An actor creating a character who waits in the darkness like a
coiled cobra, must avoid the temptation of an intellectual understanding of the metaphor: "Oh yes, coiled like a cobra; I understand
that." General intellectual comprehension often leads to generalized
emotional responses. These are of little real use to an actor until

they have been translated into motivated behavior, or until the sensory response mechanisms have been allowed to "think about" them. Metaphor should be turned into actual behavior if it is to be of direct use to your actor self. Actually turn yourself into a cobra, coiled, in the darkness, motivated to strike at the first signs of movement. Smell the air with your tongue; lift your head on the powerful, supple spine.

Start the creative forces going and learn to recognize when you must simply let the metaphor take over. You will know when you are no longer trying to respond as a cobra, trying to "stay in character", conscious of monitoring every move. Let the cobra metaphor happen to you; let yourself respond; and let it happen.

When your muscles and nerves respond effortlessly with the cobra motivation, gradually become human. Slowly stand up, allowing the motivated spine of the cobra to assume your form. Let yourself discover the dramatic character who is like a cobra by letting yourself see, hear, and respond kinesthetically with the now-human cobra's motivated senses.

Avoid generalized attitudinal responses, which will always be stereotypical. Seek direct, motivated behavior, which will never be stereotypical even when it is instantly recognizable.

The following are selected descriptions of the major character in the novel by Patrick Suskind. Take several passages and turn them into illustrative behavior by just playing actively with the rich descriptive metaphors. Don't worry whether what you are doing is right or wrong; just explore the idea of turning written metaphor into motivated behavior:

He was as tough as a resistant bacterium and as content as a tick sitting quietly on a tree and living off a tiny drop of blood plundered years before....He decided in favor of life out of sheer spite and sheer malice....he did decide vegetatively, as a bean when once tossed aside must decide whether it ought to germinate or had better let things be. Or like that tick in the tree, for which life has nothing better to offer than perpetual hibernation. The ugly little tick, which by rolling its blue-grey body up into a ball, offers the least possible surface to the world; which by making its skin smooth and dense emits nothing, lets not the tiniest bit of perspiration escape. The tick, which makes itself extra small and inconspicuous so that no one will see it and step on it. The lonely tick which, wrapped up in itself, huddles in its tree, blind, deaf and dumb, and simply sniffs, sniffs all year long, for miles around, for the blood of some passing animal that it could never reach under its own power. The tick could let itself drop. It could fall to the floor of the forest and creep a millimetre or two here or there on its six tiny legs and lie down to die under the leaves—it would be no great loss, God knows. But the tick, stubborn, sullen and loathsome, huddles there and lives and waits. Waits, for that most improbable of chances that will bring blood, in animal form, directly beneath its tree. And only then does it abandon caution and drop and scratch and bore and bite into that alien flesh....The young Grenouille [What does the name mean?] was such a tick. He lived encapsulated in himself and waited for better times. He gave the world nothing but his dung—no smile, no cry, no glimmer in the eye, not even his own scent....They didn't want to touch him. He disgusted them the way a fat spider that you can't bring yourself to crush with your own hand disgusts you.....The days of his hibernation were over. Grenouille the tick stirred again. He caught the scent of morning. He was seized with an urge to hunt. The greatest preserve for odours in the world stood open before him: the city of Paris.

Animals

Sir Laurence Olivier's 1945 production of Oedipus Rex and the moment of Oedipus' realization of the truth, provided this reaction from critic John Mason Brown:

They are the dreadful, hoarse groans of a wounded animal. They well up out of a body that has been clubbed by fate. They are sounds which speak, as no words could, for a soul torn by horror, for a mind numbed by what it as been forced to comprehend. Yet fearful as these groans are in their brute savagery, they serve only to magnify the stature of Oedipus's kingly woe. ("Olivier Comes into His Own," *Dramatis Personae*, Viking Press, 1965, p. 207.)

Olivier describes his work this way in John Mortimer's *In Character* (Penguin):

"You know what I had to do to make that pain sound real? I had to think of animals. I thought of foxes screaming, with their paws caught in the teeth of a trap." He held out his wrists, stiff and helpless. "And then I heard about how they catch ermine. It was a great help to me when I heard about that."

"How do they catch ermine?"

"You don't know?" Lord Olivier looked at me in amazement. "In the Arctic they put down salt and the ermine comes to lick it." He became a small, thirsty animal. "And his tongue freezes to the ice. I thought about that when I screamed as Oedipus."

What Olivier meant by "thought about" included a kinesthetic re-living of the thinking body, quite apart from a purely intellectual process.

• • •

Start with what the animal does, with what motivates it. Get to the essential behavior, the fundamental motivation. Go to a zoo. Study the animals in muscles and senses. Let yourself come to understand them, to be able not simply to imitate well, but to come to a muscles-and-senses understanding, to be able to respond as if you were a lion; to be able to let your spine move like the lion, walk like the lion, and your head turn like the lion. Do this until you can, without any conscious control, let yourself respond effortlessly as the animal responds and with the motivational force that organically necessitates such behavior. (It's still the same principle as learning to ride a bicycle, do a dance step, or practice a forehand in tennis until you can do it "instinctively.") At a zoo, unfortunately, we get the spine and the responses of animals that have been caged rather than the true animal, but we must take our sources where we find them.

Test with stimuli: someone throws a piece of food toward you, but at first you can't quite reach it. Is your response happening effortlessly or is some part of you still holding back and trying to decide how you should respond? Trust yourself, trust your senses and your organs of sensory response. Let them observe, perceive, respond. Motivation, the why behind the behavior remains your goal.

When you have become comfortable with the impulses and responses of you-the-lion, slowly let yourself become a human lion.

Your spine, your attitude, your sensory responses stay the same as the lion's, but you become fully human. Let an "impala person" interact. What happens? Then, two chimp people join the group. Note responses and alterations from your own habitual behavior. If you are working in a class, have a cocktail party in which all interact as their "animal people."

Hume Cronyn:

I did a lot of my preparatory study for *The Miser* on Children's Bay Cay....I was making notes when I saw the crab....he had an olive-black shell, white pincers tucked nearly beneath his body, and a gaudy orange trim about other parts of him. He was trying to pretend he wasn't visible. "Go away, I'm not here." I put out a cautious finger and touched the back of his shell. "How dare you!" He immediately sprang to attention, his multiple legs bowing under his saucer-shaped body, his pincers immediately *en garde*. I reached for a twig and flipped him over on his back....His undershell was bright orange. He had a struggle getting right side up again, but then darted toward me with the mandible of his hugely disproportioned claws spread wide. "One more indignity of that sort and I'll pinch the hell out of you!"

But it was only a demonstration charge, no sooner started than finished, and he began to creep backward. I waved my right hand and he danced to my left; waved my left hand and he scurried to my right; retreating a little every time but always threatening. "You son of a bitch, what did I ever do to you?" In the desperate retreat to his burrow he went backward over a stone, lost his balance and ended upside down again. He was ludicrous, hostile, terrified.

And I suddenly realized that I'd found a physical image for Harpagon. The terror, the threats, that evasive dancing scuttle, those bowlegs, even the color scheme...." (Vol.8, No.4., p.30, "Hume and Comedy")

Cronyn used the adjectives "ludicrous," "hostile," "terrified" and says he "found a physical image." As Cronyn described the crab to the interviewer, he was actually becoming the crab in motivated behavior terms. The "how-dare-you's" and other imaginary exclamations from the crab were abstractions that he translated into motivated responses to specific stimuli, weaving an entire complex of character behavior.

Objects

Inanimate objects and non-animal organisms are also motivated to take action. There are designed to fulfill certain goals.

• What is a teddy bear designed to do? Its motivation is expressed in spine, in arms (Why are a teddy bear's arms always open and outstretched?), a face full-front with wide open eyes. When you do these things, what do you discover about what motivates a teddy bear? Do you know someone like a teddy bear?

Explore with several objects from the same family:

• Become a rapier sword. What does it do? Let your spine become the spine of a rapier. What is a rapier motivated or designed to do? It whisks out of its scabbard; it springs flexibly into action. It sweeps and cuts the air precisely. It thrusts, it parries, it slashes, points and punctures, with speed and surprise. Let yourself do it. What happens to your voice as you let it become part of the motivated rapier sword behavior?

When you are responding freely as a rapier, work for clarification through contrast:

• Try a dagger, then a switchblade, a broadsword. Do you know someone who is like a rapier, or someone who acts like a switchblade? What motivates a switchblade?

What broadsword behavior leads you to Macbeth? Be specific. Why is Macbeth ill at ease holding a dagger, standing alone in a hallway in his castle late at night, waiting for Lady Macbeth to signal him with the ring of a bell to slip into the king's bedroom and stab him? Where does a broadsword feel most at home? Doing what?

• What does the phrase "rapier wit" imply about Mercutio's behavior?

The characters from *Everyman* give us wonderful opportunities to work with metaphor. For instance, Knowledge. Perhaps you associate with the "Tree of Knowledge." The tree is a wonderful metaphor provided that it takes you into action. What does a tree (of Knowledge) do? It reaches out, reaches up; it shelters; it grows; it sways; it bends (but does not break); it whispers and moans; it protects from sun and storm. Think of the redwoods of the West: They tower, true and strong and everlasting.

Having found these verbs what should the actor do? Avoid thinking subjectively; let yourself literally reach, tower, and shelter. Do it in dance or song until the mighty metaphor possesses you and Knowledge reaches out to a whole world.

Then work with "The Light of Knowledge."

Work to develop the metaphorizing sensibility as a natural response. Study that person who always sits in the corner of the cafeteria. What does he remind you of: A calculator? A bear? How? What does a calculator do? What motivates a bear? Expressed in what specific behavior? Study his responses, his actions. What in him reveals the bear in spine, in weight placement, in hands, in resistance to gravity? What in a bear (Have you truly perceived a bear?) reveals him?

Work from object to person, from person to object until you automatically make such metaphoric connections. Always think and work in terms of motivated action, not with adjectives or qualities or attitudes, which invariably obscure simple reality with your own biases.

Spend time each day discovering something about someone you see by finding a metaphor to clarify perceived behavior.

Drama

• Become an eagle. Sense the strength of your spine as you prepare to fly. Feel the strength in your powerful wings as you lift off into the sky. Soar to the highest reaches of a cliff. Swoop above it and sail above your kingdom.

• Now become a vulture. Grab onto a twisted limb. Fold your wings against you. Hunch up your back. Smell rotting meat in the distance. Take off in its direction. Circle the carcass, then dive for it. Scrabble around the carrion searching for a good place to rip off a chunk.

Look into the sky and see an eagle; let your spine and muscles want to be an eagle.

• Richard III is a hunched-over vulture whose spine strains to soar like an eagle. Try it. Let him try to turn his twisted vulture spine into the spine of an eagle. What discoveries do you make about Richard's spine, or his voice? Where is the drama of opposing forces?

• Nina is a soaring sea gull who touches the air currents with the tips of her fingers, rides the currents around the lake in safety. What motivates this graceful gull? What happens when she leaves the lake and a storm comes? (Masha senses a storm coming in Act I. It finally comes, in stage time, between Acts III and IV.)

• Treplev wants to soar, but what is the opposite force at work on him?

• Marchbanks is a frightened stray puppy with a brilliant mind. Have you ever seen a stray puppy cringe and shrink from being touched? Why? Apply to Marchbanks. What discoveries do you make?

Actually doing the animals and exploring the metaphor in motivated behavioral terms, is a shortcut to getting your muscles and senses to understand the metaphoric character. The behavior of the stray puppy is true of Marchbanks, too. Add the fiery eyes ablaze with ideas aimed at puncturing hypocrisy; the mind that seethes with the poet's capacity to see into the human condition. Look at Shaw's description of Marchbanks' entrance in Act I.

• Hedda is associated with her father's duelling pistols. Turn the qualities of a duelling pistol into motivated action by exploring what it actually does and what it is designed to do. Respond to an actual pistol by lifting it, hefting it. Come to experience its craftsmanship, its perfect balance, its sleek lines. Aim it. If you can, fire it. Respond to it until something of the pistol has taken over in your own responses. Then work deliberately: A duelling pistol is designed to fire a bullet at a target some distance away with force and accuracy. To achieve this motivation, it is perfectly balanced; its sleek lines suggest a straight spine free of extraneous distractions. It cocks and the internal spring tightens before the bullet fires. Let your totality explore these ideas: What if I were a duelling pistol? What if I were balanced (move, respond, walk, turn in perfect balance) and if there were no extraneous lines or decorations? (What implications are there for behavior, in spine, shoulders, chest, pelvis?) What if I tightened (in the spine?) to explode? Hedda has lovely balance in sleek lines. She has no extraneous, fussy Victorian touches to her clothes. Let the pistol metaphor suggest something about her stance, her walk. Discover implications in her spine as the hammer is cocked and the spring in the pistol tightens with slow pressure on the trigger.

• Now add the opposite that leads to Hedda: What if I feared laughing, gossiping voices? Imagine (become, do) a cocked pistol, the trigger tightening to fire; it will not let people know and so it turns away, squeezes to shoot, laughs in an effort to disguise what is really happening. Through it all, there is no release from the pressure that eventually forces it to fire. (Where is the irony in Hedda's shooting herself?)

Notice that you stay with what the object actually does and the why of that behavior. Avoid imposing your own prejudices: A pistol is motivated to murder; a pistol is dangerous and evil. Focus rather on what actual behavior is perceived as dangerous and evil. Stay simply, literally, with what it is designed (motivated) to do, with what it actually does. Other people may see what it does as dangerous or evil, but that's of little help to the actor trying to embody the character.

Hedda is also associated with horses. Perhaps she is a wild mare who cannot bear being corralled. Play with that metaphor until you discover not only Hedda's trapped spine but some of the opposite resistance to that caged reality.

• Lopakhin is a Peasant (Literalize "Strong as an ox.") with a Businessman's sensibility and a Great Dane puppy's love for Lubov. In Gaev's house he becomes a bull in a china shop. All this infused with the soul of an artist.

Create the Russian peasant spine: Mend a fence; feed the pigs; chop wood. Study photos of Brezshnev when he visited the

Nixon White House. There is a series of photos in *Time* magazine taken of a champagne toast being spilled over the hands of both men. It is a priceless evocation of Lopakhin in a cultured environment foreign to his experience. Study these photos. Take that spine and tramp through the cherry orchard. Study the big peasant hands as they try to drink champagne (You'll need it for Act IV). There are photos of Brezshnev and Nixon riding in an electric golf cart. All emerge in response to the activating stimuli that say "Russian Peasant."

Now activate the businessman's mind and spine that can see money-making possibilities. It is always helpful to start with yourself or already-perceived people: the man you know from the construction site who has moved up from laborer to head of his own company. He scouts out the land, sees possibility, talks to his foreman. "We can level that small hill and extend the road from there...." Do this to allow your totality an opportunity to explore the idea of "self-made businessman" in terms of improvised motivated behavior. When you are comfortably responding, add him to the Russian peasant spine.

Then play with the Great Dane puppy metaphor. Actually become a Great Dane puppy. Play, jump, fetch a ball, leap up and lick the face of your human friend and throw your clumsy paws on her until you are responding freely with a puppy's spontaneously motivated spine. Incorporate him into your peasant who has the mind of a businessman. How? Just let him be there. He will spontaneously emerge in response to the proper stimuli; in Lopakhin's case, the moment Lubov enters the room.

Do the same with The Bull in a China Shop. Go back to Brezshnev.

The artistic sense: Lopakhin looks out over a field of poppies, sees a train puffing away in the distance. Something about Russia and Russians stirs his soul, but he is an uneducated, inarticulate peasant who cannot let the feelings play through. Instead he laughs too loudly, scratches his arm self-consciously, kicks a stone, or in the case of the moment in Act II, simply stands awkwardly, staring, a bit embarrassed, and then manages a loud, "We should be giants." Why does he wave his arms about?

When I was studying with Alvina Krause, I worked part-time at a fast food restaurant. A young man in his late-twenties came in frequently to socialize with the high school kids who hung out there. Charlie had dropped out of high school, joined the military and had recently returned from Vietnam. He was having trouble finding a steady job and wasn't sure what it was he wanted to do. He and I became friends partly because we were both a bit too old to be at the restaurant. Perhaps he sensed in the twenty-five year old fryer of hamburgers a fellow lost soul.

After work, Charlie would often drive me to a favorite spot in the country. We would get out of the car, sit under a tree and look up into the night sky. We rarely spoke. When he did, he would say things like, "So many stars. There has to be life out there somewhere." Pause. "You could get lost out there." Always chewing on the side of his index finger or tossing stones into the grass beyond us. A voice unsure of itself, unable even to play implication beyond the words. But somewhere inside him dwelt the need of the poetic temperament to express itself.

Something in Charlie's eyes, something in the struggle his heart had with trying to find the right words, the right delicate vocal quality, evokes the Lopakhin of Act II who tries to express something of his response to Mother Russia: "We should be giants." Somewhere deep inside the awkward peasant who gets frustrated when Gaev and Lubov can't see things from his business point of view; somewhere behind the inability to find the words or appropriate tone of voice when he comes face to face with Varya, there is a poet like the poet who had a hard time expressing himself inside the uneducated, inarticulate Charlie.

The deepest self of Lopakhin is the peasant; the peasant develops the businessman's sensibilities, manifested most directly in his eyes and a tone of voice. When Lubov appears, the clumsy Great Dane puppy that Lopakhin was as a child is activated. When he puts on respectable suits and new shoes and comes into Gaev's house, the peasant/businessman becomes the bull in the china shop. When he sees a sunset, or watches farmers working in a field, the poet in him comes alive. The voice is always the booming, inexpressive peasant voice even if the words struggle with artistic sensibility. Lopakhin is a most complex human being. He could be Chekhov's Caliban.

Not all behavior that is associated with the metaphorizer is necessarily revelatory. Learn to let the play help you ask the right questions in order to set your imagination going in the right direction. One critic interpreted Nina in *The Sea Gull* (and consequently the entire play) from the single observation that sea gulls are scavengers: They prey on carrion, they screech; they squawk; they are stupid, awkward, nasty-tempered animals. Since Nina is associated with the sea gull, Nina becomes exclusively identified in the critic's mind as a predatory, scavenging young vampire who will be worse than Arkadina ever was.

How can we tell from the context of the play what specific motivated behavior of the sea gull Chekhov had in mind when he lets Nina say, "I am drawn to this lake like a sea gull"? With what other significant elements in the play does the sea gull image resonate?

Your personal response to the metaphor (whether or not you like stray puppies, or how you feel about a pistol), is not important. Rather: What motivates the behavior? What other clues and nuances does the playwright give? Why did the playwright include this element in the play?

Opposites

Always look for opposites. If the man in the cafeteria is a bear, what opposite plays against these actions, to compensate or balance? Might there be a butterfly in him too, or a child?

• Tesman is a researcher, a mouse nibbling on scraps of information. But he is also a loveable pair of old slippers, comfortable, curling up in a chair. He is a person an old maiden aunt would adore; but a Hedda?

• Hedda is a pistol. What is her opposite? In great drama, the obvious opposite often leads to triteness. Hedda the pistol versus Hedda the rag doll? Probably not. What about Hedda the pistol as opposed to the aristocrat, or the Victorian lady? The coward afraid of gossip and scandal? Which is the Hedda that most people see and respond to? What clues does the play offer? Test yourself: Be one of the townspeople who sees Hedda in front of her house. What is she doing? Does she spend time sitting in a swing? Do you see her in the garden cutting flowers? Does she take leisurely walks through her neighborhood? Aunt Julie remembers seeing Hedda dressed in her black riding habit passing by on her horse.

• What does Judge Brack see, in literal details, when he looks at Hedda? The curve of her breast, the long line of her neck, a foot tapping, eyes that look beyond? Is she a bored woman who needs stimulation in her life?

• What does Tesman see, or Thea, or Lovborg? Be specific.

You have within you a pistol, a mouse, a peacock. What touches off the mouse in you? What circumstances trigger the duelling pistol? In response to what stimuli does the peacock within unfold? Bring a duelling pistol to life; create a peacock and a then create a mouse. Let them interact. In a conflict among these three, which one should logically prevail? What do you discover about the ironies of the drama in the metaphorized relationships among Hedda, Brack and Tesman?

• Play with these contrasts: Candida the mother, Eugene the stray puppy, Morell the minister. What are the Morell opposites? Can you find a metaphor to express them? Metaphorize the Morell who grabs Marchbanks toward the end of Act I and nearly throttles him. The child in Morell comes out most clearly in Act II when Candida says, "Jealous for somebody else, who is not loved as he ought to be," and the little boy inside Morell says hopefully, "Me?" It's delightful.

• Along these lines, create the opposites of the characters from *The Sea Gull.*

• Explore *Romeo and Juliet* from this point of view.

• Macbeth the soldier, the poet, wants to possess the throne.

1. Honor, integrity, decency as opposed to Base Ambition.

2. The eagle versus what?

Metaphor and Relationships

There are implications beyond the animal or object which illuminate character motivation. Relationships can also be clarified by imaginative use of metaphor.

Improvise each of the following, taking note of behavior expressive of the relationship. Transfer the behavior to a specific illustration of the dramatic relationship.

• Mother/nurturer and a stray puppy. What do you discover happens between the two? Let them become Candida and Marchbanks as they get ready to go away for the weekend before the play starts. Can you add: Stray puppy with a poet's heart imagines the mother is a saint?

• A fat old tabby cat: Motivation? Put it in a big country kitchen. Let it have a bed against the wall near the stove. Is there fresh milk in the pan? A frisky kitten: Motivation? Get a ball of yarn or a butterfly. Let the yarn roll right up to the sleeping tabby cat.

What do you discover when you improvise these two in their relationship with each other? Apply it improvisationally to the Nurse and Juliet.

• How might you metaphorize the relationship between Arkadina and Treplev?

• Lady Macbeth watches Macbeth like a hawk. (I am reminded of photos of Nancy Reagan standing behind Ronald Reagan with a smile on her lips but hawk eyes surveying the surroundings to intercept any difficulty.)

Situation

It helps to find a metaphor for the situation of a play:

• Hamlet is a sane young man in a world that has gone mad; the rules change constantly. Let you-Hamlet act out the changes in the rules that govern human relationships: Wife and husband; friend to friend; mother and son. Let yourself metaphorize the changes or demonstrate what has happened to the rules of kingly governance in metaphoric terms. Trap doors suddenly open where there weren't trap doors before. A ghost appears on the battlements and people spring out from behind arrases where they have been spying. Give more metaphoric examples as Hamlet doing a show-and-tell of what the world has become for him.

• Create an engaging metaphor for the underlying situation behind *The Cherry Orchard*.

• It's easy to misread the situation of *Candida*. Devise a metaphor to illustrate clearly.

Fantasy

You perceive people in response to the stimuli of their world. You come to sensory comprehension of the why behind behavior. You study sensory responses as they reveal motivation. You discover the centrality of the spine in the manifestation of motivating drive. You study animals and objects. You learn to view all natural phenomena as sources of understanding motivation through metaphor. You learn to bring vicarious experience to your creative imagination: music, painting, photography, books. Now let's put it all together.

Create a list that contains groups of three elements, usually a person, an object, an animal. Explore the implications of the relationship among the elements by "becoming" one of them. For instance: actress, mirror, puppy. On the simplest, most basic level, what motivates an actress? Create the spine of an actress in an environment that most directly activates such motivated behavior. When you are responding freely and naturally, let the mirror come into the situation. Let yourself respond and discover what motivates a mirror. What is it designed to do? Create a fundamental dramatic relationship between your actress and the mirror. Next, bring the puppy into the situation. What motivates a puppy, and how is that manifested in direct behavior? Discover the drama inherent in the interaction of an actress, a mirror, and a puppy.

At this stage, there need be no story or plot governing your discoveries. This is instead the "thinking through" stage in terms of action, behavior and response. Let the situation play itself out. It might be of benefit for someone else to play the puppy to contribute new possibilities.

When you have played through the situation's possibilities, come at it from the point of view of a puppy. Respond with a puppy's motivation and in a puppy's world, then add the other elements one at a time as you explore and discover.

Keep the motivations, the "character" as simple and as direct as possible. Avoid creating undue complexities; for example, a puppy who doesn't trust anyone but is desperately needful of finding a home, or an actress who is terrified of her public and only wants to make it through the performance so that she can get to her liquor cabinet. These ideas will only blur the point, which is to explore in the purest, most fundamental form the notion of a motivated spine; response to significant stimuli; consequent relationship with other elements; drama in the direct clash of forces.

After working through the elements in this manner, choose one of the protagonists and create a simple narrative. The drama must depend upon the clashing motivations of the three elements. (Why must it be a puppy and not a kitten in order for your story to happen? Why a mirror?)

The story should be largely non-verbal so that sensory behavioral interaction becomes the basis of drama, not dialogue. Focus on the active process of dramatizing the essentials rather than the passive process of revelation through conversation.

A minimal use of props is suggested; use pantomimic response to create reality as ordinary or as fantastic as you wish. You will discover the natural logic of any drama; you can create any form of believable reality once you discover the logical rules that govern that reality and you behave according to them. These speculations form the necessary beginning work on creating the world of the play for an audience.

Create a fantasy drama using these combinations:

- Actress, mirror, puppy
- Soldier, devil, rose
- Farmer, mermaid, window
- Child, butterfly, axe
- Doctor, skull, orchid
- Eagle, window, crown
- Child, computer, dungeon
- Mother, wounded deer, cave
- Tramp, pig, tree

Some of these fantasies are suggested by actual plays. For example, Actress, mirror, puppy is based on the relationship between Arkadina and Treplev and is particularly applicable to the bandage scene of Act III. But many narratives are possible; for example, an actress uses her mirror as part of her work process as she auditions for the role of a puppy. Or, a puppy keeps coming up to the mirror to check himself, then dashes off to the wings to make sure he hasn't missed something. He returns to the dressing room where the actress enters to give him instructions, until finally he pads offstage with great confidence. From behind the curtain we hear a bright clear voice singing "Tomorrow" from Annie! Anything is possible.

The fantasy work helps to illustrate fundamental principles of acting: What are motivation, relationship, interaction? Is something perceivable actually happening or are you creating emotional, passive people who simply watch what is happening? How do you discover the internal logic of any narrative? How do you tell a story? What is the nature of dramatic suspense? Metaphor helps you to actualize all of these elements. Of course, after these essential principles have been assimilated, feel free to add complexity and invent your own variations on the exercise. But stick with the fundamentals first.

When you are studying plays, do the process in reverse. Consider the play's significant elements in action terms then let your imagination play with motivations and potentials for dramatic conflict until you discover the play's essence.

• Candida—mother, minister, poet/stray puppy/child, fireplace. What motivates a mother? What's important to a minister? What does a stray puppy want? What if the puppy has the soul of a poet? Why a fireplace? What motivates a fireplace? Does the phrase "hearth and home" apply? What's the irony? What part does the fireplace play in dramatizing each act of Candida? What might happen if the confrontation that ends the play occurred in a bedroom? What if all the characters met in a garden and a fountain was the most significant environmental element? (Avoid quick intellectual responses to these questions. Explore the possibilities in action as you explored the implications of the elements in the fantasy work.) Note the use of the fireplace throughout the play. What part does it play in activating Morell's character in the early scene with Burgess? What change happens in the way Candida and Marchbanks respond to it at the beginning of Act III? What specific responses does Shaw suggest for Candida with the fireplace during that final confrontation? (Later, when Candida decides it is time for the men in her life to learn a lesson, she goes to the fireplace, puts her foot up on the fender, leans her elbow on the mantle.) At the end of the play, Marchbanks leaves happiness, hearth and home to go into the night, where something nobler waits him. What is the secret in the poet's heart?

• Why does *The Sea Gull* happen at a lake and not a riverfront? What if Lubov's son Grisha had drowned in a lake rather than a river? *The Cherry Orchard* would be a different play if it took place near a lake; *The Sea Gull* a different play if the house were situated on a big river. (What does a lake "do"? What "motivates" a river?)

• Why, in terms of drama, does the fog surround the house in *Long Day's Journey into Night?*

The fantasy asks you to create motivation simply, clearly, and in direct terms of active response to specific stimuli. It asks you to discover why significant elements are included in a play. Human motivations clash with one another and with environmental motivations and drama happens. (One of the reasons *The Sea Gull* functions with such strong conflicting undercurrents is that Arkadina's driven star spine is dramatized in an environment with few of the stimuli that activate and nourish that driving force. The most powerful character spine in the play is put into direct opposition to the very forces of the play's environment.)

As you actively explore each element to discover what each does and why, your imagination can play freely through the creation of conflict, opposition, and drama. This can lead to gentle humor, the profoundest tragedy, fantastic imaginary worlds, or the most realistic evocation of daily life. Learn how to discover the active motivations and situations that touch off direct opposition, and you will have taken a giant step forward toward understanding why playwrights arrange their people, objects and environments the way they do. You will be developing your imagination as a boundlessly creative power in your work as an actor.

The Novel

Every novel has a narrative voice that determines the point of view from which the story will be read. It selects what details of character, situation, and action, must be revealed in what order and with what emphasis. Every play also posseses an organizing narrative voice in the shape of the ensemble of actors who perform it. They take the place of the playwright and share in clearly communicating the play's point of view to the audience.

Novelists can select and reveal many more details to their reader than playwrights can to their audience: What characters are doing as they speak, what they are thinking but not saying, what other responses they are having, and so on. Playwrights count on actors to supply those revealing details and to become novelists in terms of actual human behavior.

So the actor might look to the novelist for guidance in developing this ability.

Choose a novel of character, for example, *Madame Bovary*, or *Middlemarch*. Let your imagination play with the given elements. Explore the title of the book, the location, and significant descriptions of locale. What other elements are emphasized as significant? Is a character's name important? What is each character doing and in what environment and with whom when the author introduces her or him? Why? What colors predominate? Is the time of year or the weather a factor? As ever, don't just let your analytical mind become involved; use your senses, your responsive behavioral urges, your imagination. Play with association, metaphor, resonances. Find the scene in *Anna Karenina* where Levin watches Kitty ice-skating. What "meaning" does ice-skating have for Kitty's character? What is its influence on what happens between Kitty and Levin?

Find passages that contain character description. Let your imagination find ways to embody these descriptions in actor's terms. The following is a description of Eustacia Vye in Thomas Hardy's *The Return of the Native*:

Eustacia Vye was the raw material of divinity. On Olympus she would have done well with a little preparation....To see her hair was to fancy that a whole winter did not contain darkness enough to form its shadow—it closed over her forehead like nightfall extinguishing the western glow...She had pagan eyes, full of nocturnal mysteries, and their light, as it came and went, and came again, was partially hampered by their oppressive lids and lashes;... Assuming that souls of men and women were visible essences, you could fancy the colour of Eustacia's soul to be flamelike. The sparks from it that rose into her dark pupils gave the same impression....Her presence brought memories of such things as Bourbon roses, rubies, and tropical midnight; her moods recalled lotus-eaters and the march in Athalie; her motions, the ebb and flow of the sea; her voice, the viola. In a dim light, and with a slight rearrangement of her hair, her general figure might have stood for that of either of the higher female deities.

Throughout the novel, Eustacia is associated with the colors red and black. Let them play upon your actor's imagination. Fire and night. Passion and concealment.

Note the appeal to music and the kinesthetic sense in Hardy's evocation of Eustacia. Find the lotos-eaters in Homer and Tennyson and read. What motivates the music of the viola? How is it produced and what is its specific effect on the listener? Find and listen to it. Let your muscles explore the implications of "the ebb and flow of the sea." Let your actor's imagination play with these descriptions and metaphors; let their suggestion play upon your senses and muscles, turning these words into illustrative response and behavior. What does the name Eustacia mean? Why "Vye"?

Choose a particularly illuminating passage from the novel, preferably when the character is alone, with little or no dialogue. Create this passage in an actor's terms of motivation, needs and desires, responding to the particular stimuli described by the novelist. Let the novelists' imagination, expressed in terms of ideas, descriptions and metaphors, spark off your actor's imagination to create the character.

• From *Return of the Native,* work to create the passage in which Eustacia is introduced. Then try the sequence of her leaving the house and building the signal fire.

• In *Oliver Twist*, read the description of Fagin's journey to Bill Syke's place as he persuades him to take Oliver on his next job. Active descriptive words, such as the final "reptile" metaphor, help the actor create.

• Study Catherine Earnshaw and Heathcliff from Emily Bronte's *Wuthering Heights*. To what does the "wuthering" refer? Bring the moor to life: the wind, the craggy mountains, the storms, the desolate house. Catherine and Heathcliff become the human embodiment of the forces of the wild country, living so violently and passionately that even death cannot keep them apart. Turn the intense extreme passages into imaginative creative behavior. Bring the raw beauty of this novel alive.

• Let your imagination play with how Tolstoy introduces Anna Karenina into the novel. Bring the tone and feel of this passage to life.

• Then try Emma Bovary watching Leon at the fair.

• Take a look at Hardy's Jude and *The Mayor of Casterbridge*.

Turn the exercise around. Convey through writing what discoveries you make about a play through its tone, its communication purpose, and the relative complexity of its characters:

• Take Natasha's entrance in *Three Sisters* and write it as part of a realistic character novel.

• Describe what happens to Hedda during her conversation with Judge Brack in Act II as though it were in a novel. Describe exactly what happens between the moment she tells him she's going to shoot him and her line: "I was only shooting into the blue."

• The first time you see Candida.

• Nora's entrance in *A Doll House*.

In each case, let yourself actually do what you wrote.

What kind of novel writing would be appropriate for describing a passage from *Waiting for Godot*, or for *The Tempest*? Does this give clues to acting that reality?

Ideas come from everywhere, not just the great nineteenth-century novels. During one recent summer I read the detective novels of P.D. James and discovered several descriptions that clarified dramatic characters for me.

Turn these descriptions from P.D. James into motivated behavior and then apply the behavior to the dramatic character.

From *Shroud for a Nightingale:*

> He brought with him an air of music hall bon hommie and, as always, a faint smell of sour sweat....He...did not easily take offense....He...adhere d to the principle that you should never willingly offend anyone, however humble...He liked himself too well to conceive that other men might find him less lovable, and this endearing naivety gave him a kind of charm....Women were said to find him attractive....his was the infectious good humor of a man who necessarily finds the world an agreeable place since it contains himself.

As an actor, what does your imagination do with "air of music hall bon hommie"? How would you illustrate "He liked himself too well...."? Apply all this to Shakespeare's Falstaff as he regales his friends in the pub. What does the Falstaff "charm" actually do? Compare with Cary Grant's "charm" in action terms.

From *An Unsuitable Job for a Woman:*

> ...Cordelia had stayed on at the convent for the six most settled and happy years of her life, insulated by order and ceremony from the mess and muddle of life outside.

Here's a beautifully compact answer to the question of Isabella's motivation in *Measure for Measure.* Put that description into illustrative behavioral terms when life intervenes and Isabella goes to the court to plead for mercy for her brother.

From *The Skull Beneath the Skin:*

> ...He sensed that he was worse than a failure, that he was the last of a series of failures, that earlier disappointments had reinforced her present discontent.

> "Please let the weekend be a success. Don't let me make a fool of myself. Please don't let the girl despise me. Please let Clarissa be in a good mood. Please don't let Clarissa throw me

out. Oh God, please don't let anything terrible happen on Coucy Island."

Increasingly he had come to feel that Clarissa repented of a generosity which at first had held all the charm of novelty, the magnificent gesture, superbly theatrical at the time in all its eccentricity but which she now saw had lumbered her with a spotty, inarticulate adolescent, ill at ease with her friends; with school bills, holiday arrangements, dental appointments, with all the minor irritations of motherhood and none of its essential compensations. He sensed that there was something she required of him which he could neither identify nor give, some return, unspecified but substantial which would one day be demanded of him with all the brutal insistence of a tax-collector.

Turn these descriptions into action. Let the words send your imagination galloping toward realizing Treplev and his relationship with Arkadina. Apply your discoveries directly to improvised moments from Treplev's life.

• • •

The playwright provides the blueprint from which the imagination takes its cues. Within the blueprint of the play, actors bring the characters, their relationships, the environment, the situation and the drama to creative imaginative life.

The exercises described in this book are simply ways for you to develop your creativity to reach that goal; to help you to ask a play to stimulate your imagination; to discover what the play is about and how it gets there; and to find out why, in actor's terms, the playwright included all the elements in the play.

As actors, your imagination works in terms of action. Develop the creative powers of your totality. Let your thinking body respond and imagine as you learn to listen to it. Never let any exercises become ends in themselves. Some will be more stimulating than others; some may even make no reasonable sense to you at all. Fine. But give everything a chance. Work to discover what each exercise is designed to illustrate. Always find other ways to illustrate the same principle in your own way and with your own exercises.

Let your mind find the words for what your being creates. Analyze and clarify only after your muscles and senses explore: That is the discipline of good acting and good theatre. Avoid giving the intellect a dictator's power, for discipline for its own sake is tyranny. Imagination without discipline is like any power without structure: dangerous, chaotic, even destructive. But imagination with discipline, the goal of all this work—that is artistic freedom.

4

Characterization

> *Your personality is the entire motivational, attitudinal, and behavioral system that characterizes your adjustment to the world. It is made up of traits, values, motives, and many other processes and constructs....All of your behavior connects up in one way or another to your personality as a product of traits, motives, and so on (inner personality characteristics) in interaction with your environment (outer situational characteristics).*
>
> — *Dan P. McAdams*, The Stories We Live By

Human Character

The actor's creative goal is to communicate to an audience what the playwright's play dramatizes about human life. Thus far, we have concerned ourselves with ways to develop the actor's essential creative capacities: the capacity to perceive and store up meaningful revelatory images of human behavior; the capacity to use the world around you, including other art forms, as fodder for your creative imagination; the capacity to read a play imaginatively for clues to its meanings and communication objectives. Now we focus on the initial creative task of the actor on the way to achieving the goal of communicating a play to an audience. Before there can be drama, there must be character of some kind. The subject of this chapter is Dramatic Characterization.

The traditional dichotomy of nature/biology and nurture/culture may serve to organize our thinking about the process of human character development. At one end of the nature-versus-nurture continuum, nature/biology includes what we consider our ancestral contribution to our creation: Genetically inherited factors such as sex and racial characteristics, height, eye and hair color, and other traits. Between the two poles of genes and environment the biochemistry of the nine-month human gestation period seems to affect such diverse elements of health and temperament as susceptibility to disease, level of creativity, affection orientation, propensity to aggression, and others, which may emerge as dispositions toward or proclivities for certain kinds of behavior. At the opposite end, nurture/culture may be thought of as the sum of our life's experiences, including actions taken to alter inherited traits. (Helen Keller's life is a triumph of such actions.)

However we may account for them, we are a lifetime of the responses we have made to our sensory stimuli: what we have seen, heard, touched, smelled, tasted and reacted to kinesthetically. We are who we are in our responses to our world. We are the books we have read and have not read. We are the music we have heard and retained until it has become a part of our very rhythms and we are the music we have not heard nor retained. We are all the places we have lived in and travelled to. We are the people we have loved or hated, turned to and run away from, accepted or rejected. We are the relationships we have developed and dissolved. We are who we are in response to the people who have accepted or rejected us, who have ignored, tolerated or threatened us. We are the successes that have lifted our spines and strengthened our hearts, the downfalls that have caved in our chests and slumped our shoulders. We are the adjustments we have made and have failed to make. We are the astonishments we have experienced and the deep realizations and significant decisions we have come to, both conscious and unconscious, because of those experiences. We are the choices we have made and the needs and desires they have engendered. We are our fears and phobias, our repulsions, our prejudices, our hopes. And we are the habitual actions we take because of all these things.

All that we are we bring to every moment of our lives. To each experience we bring our totality. We bring images and associations that play through our senses and our muscles, that become part of those forces that carry us along. We bring the unspoken concerns and concealed preoccupations that play beneath the surface of our lives, occasionally bursting through the surface into words and immediate action.

Each individual's basic character drive or essential motivated spine has emerged from and has been forged by a complex background of the active, powerful forces of their individual world.

In order to discover how you became who you are, explore the world from which you emerged.

• The forces of nature/biology:

What traits did you inherit? Include the factors associated with pre-natal biology, (allergies, tendency toward stress, illness) and those that may be influenced by both poles of the nature/nurture continuum (artistic sensitivities, athletic prowess, sexuality).

• The forces of nurture/culture:

What environmental forces have influenced your development? What moral, economic, social, religious, political, cultural, and intellectual forces? Try to be as specific as possible.

• People sometimes consider the influence of nature/biology and of nurture/culture as interchangeable:

"Alcoholism runs in their family."

"She inherited her love of horses from her mother."

"Men in that family have always been gamblers."

From the actor's point of view, regardless of which side of the nature-versus-nurture dichotomy a character trait lies, it must be created in terms of motivated behavior. Let us examine fundamental questions of psychology, philosophy, and biology from the actor's point of view until we account for all of the determining factors of human endeavor which created you.

• The first goal is to establish the major forces of actual human interaction that underpin an individual's world.

I am a post-World War II baby-boomer from a specific socio-economic class. Among the influences that an actor would need to create my background world are these:

1. Suburbs and housing developments in formerly agricultural areas outside of cities and towns (miniature ranch-style houses, newly-planted shrubbery and trees, where everyone is a new neighbor for everyone else).
2. The growth of the steel industry and the nation's highways.
3. The growing idea of providing college education for all and its impact on the conflict between the generations, especially in working class families.
4. The domination of rock and roll.
5. The Cold War and the fear of Communism and nuclear destruction (every Saturday I went to see the latest movie about giant insects mutated from nuclear testing), versus the exhilarating feeling that America, with the end of World War II, ruled the world and could do no wrong. (President Eisenhower, speaking of the Soviet Union, said, "How can you talk to a nation of peasants?" Huge American automobiles sail down broad city streets and nationwide super highways. "Made in Japan" printed on anything causes outburst of laughter and jingoistic jokes.)

The child of the late forties and early fifties became a young man in the sixties and the Vietnam era. Books, film and video documentaries, and photographic essays will help to bring to life the influences of such national experiences.

Set up the era from which you emerge by creating, in terms of actual human interaction, the major influential currents of the time.

If you are an American in your late teens or early twenties today, you share your similarities of background influence with all the children of baby-boomers. The optimism of the America that helped create you was profoundly shaken by the assassinations of John F. and Robert Kennedy and Martin Luther King. The America from which you emerged was created in part by the wrenching national conflicts of the Vietnam war. Even if you were not alive when America witnessed the assassinations of its leaders and the consequent distrust of all political and governmental agencies; even if you were not alive while America engaged in the Vietnam war, you are partially who you are because those experiences had an effect on the Americans who became your parents and families. In discussing her parents' disapproval of her taking part in a pro-Choice march, one of my students said recently, "My parents were my age in 1968; you'd think they'd understand this."

Devise improvisations that illustrate the character capacities that this student expects people who were twenty years old in the sixties to share. How can you speculate about such determining influences from your own experience?

Illustrate the world from which you emerged. For each factor, devise significant illustrative improvisations. Discover, in experiential terms, the major forces that shape anyone emerging from your background.

• Move to narrower spheres to further individuate the specific background realities that create the person who will become you.

To create a character who will become David Downs, for instance, actors would need to create a Western Pennsylvania mining town in the early fifties with these characteristics:

1. Mostly Eastern European immigrants (What does this mean in terms of human interaction?)
2. Roman Catholic school and church. (pre Pope John XXIII)
3. Economics and occupation (former mine workers, now laborers in steel mills. D.H. Lawrence's *Sons and Lovers*, although it is set in turn-of-the-century England, gives terrific sensory and experiential details to describe such a life)
4. Duplex company houses (outside plumbing, no hot water, all children sleep in the same small room, etc.).

Set up speculative improvisations to illustrate in actors' terms, what it means to be a post-World War II child who grew up in such an environment.

Notice that the mining town improvisations do not yet focus on the experiences that were specifically mine or immediately involved in forming my unique individuality. This stage of the improvisations create the social, economic, religious and cultural forces that will determine the character of all people developing in these environments. We simply establish the typical experiences and shared interactions that create the world of a post-World War II Pennsylvania mining town.

What part of the country do you come from? Illustrate its influence on creating human character. Be specific: Manhattan versus Iowa farmland. Let a native of Manhattan show what it means to live in Manhattan (the stimuli that make certain kinds of behavior become "typical" of the Manhattanite); let a smalltown Iowan demonstrate typical (not to say stereotypical) developmental experiences. How does where you currently live play its part in creating a Someone who will eventually become you? The following are actual examples from my students' lives:

1. A young man from the east coast whose family has ties with organized crime demonstrates experiences from his grandfather's life, his father's life and his own life that illustrate the ruling premise of his family: "Blood (family) first."
2. A young man from the hills of Tennessee whose grandfather was Creek Indian.
3. A young woman from a Greek Orthodox family living on Long Island.
4. A young African-American woman whose father served in the military and who grew up on a German military base.
5. A young Jewish woman who grew up in Switzerland and Japan where her father headed the cardiac units of several hospitals.
6. A young gay man from a Polish working-class Chicago neighborhood.

• Consider next the family biographical phase, the final individualizing phase of the persons who emerge from this background. Remember that you are trying to get the actor creating your character to experience the reality, not merely to respond emotionally.

Your work on the immediate individualizing environmental improvisations is guided by these considerations:

1. Illustrate in behavioral terms the dominant influence exerted by mother, father, siblings, relatives and extended family. Demonstrate the nature of parental discipline and nurturing in your world and in your immediate family: physical, emotional, sexual and psychological aspects. Has there been separation or divorce? Why or why not? With what effect on character?

2. What influence have financial concerns had on a family level? Illustrate. Career and occupation: A friend of mine recently said that the difference between him and his parents was that he has a career but his parents had jobs. Illustrate the effect that your father's and your mother's occupations have on the family and on creating you. Be specific. How are father and/or mother dressed when they come home from work? What is the first thing each does when entering the house? Why? With what effect on the developing you?

3. Consider the extent of and attitude toward education in your family.

4. Consider the place of religion.

5. Was there access travel and to what extent?

6. What kinds of magazines lie around your house?

7. Illustrate the breadth of concerns, of understanding of the world. How was this generated? (I have an eighty-five-year-old aunt who has lived her entire life in the Pennsylvania mining town where she was born. At the time my sister was offered a job in Texas, my aunt asked, "Which Texas? There are two Texases, aren't there? Dallas and Houston.")

8. Attitudes toward leisure time, games and sports. When is the television on? What kind of vacations does your family take? Why?

9. Attitude toward alcohol and drugs, toward sex and sexuality, gender issues, race, nationality.
10. What importance does your family place on the arts? With what effect on character?
11. Political concerns.
12. Environmental concerns.
13. The nature of family rituals: meal time, vacations, "event" parties (graduation, birthday), weekend rituals, bedtime.

Many factors contribute to the development of human character. These paragraphs have been intended only to spark your thinking. Use your own lives and the lives of people you know to expand these ideas. Imagine in terms of human incident all of the experiences that go into creating the world from which you developed. The goal: to account for all the factors that result in the developing human being and to do so in illustrative actors' terms, in terms of sensory specifics: How are these things manifested in terms of human interaction? What would a stranger entering your world experience that would express the reality of each of these factors?

• Arrive at statements of the opposing forces that underpin your world; for example:

1. Honor thy father and thy mother versus To thine own self be true
2. You must get an education versus Live while you can
3. Make the family proud of you versus Follow your own star
4. Religion says—? versus My social needs say—? versus My inner voice says—?
5. I want to—? versus I fear—?
6. I need to—? versus I want to—?

Illustrate these ideas, tailoring the examples to your life, how your family affected the developing you. Add significant oppositions that apply specifically to you and your world. Speculate, improvise and give examples in real, literal and interactive terms. In this way, the actor "thinks through," from a behavioral standpoint, ideas about the development of human character. Work improvisationally until you can perceive the dynamic forces that underpin the world as dramatic oppositions, as conflicting forces, as the dynamic tension between positive choices, as realizations and decisions which form character.

Basic Driving Force

From the infinite variety of stimuli and responses that create your world, what are the most crucial to the emerging you? Between opposing sets of stimuli to which your character is alternately attracted and repelled, some become more important than others. You make decisions that strengthen certain impulses in you, and that further develop your motivating spine. What becomes most important? Why?

What stimuli strengthen the developing spine of you? What bends it, pushes down on it? What accounts for your range of interests; the extent of your world awareness and your curiosity? What about your relationships with others? What do you run away from? What do you embrace? Why? What are the forces that support that drive? What factors suppress it? How did all this happen? Of all the forces playing in your world, which have become the basic drive of your brother? sister? How do you account for the fact that your basic drives are different even though you've grown up in the same specific environment?

Character is an ongoing interactive stimulus/response process of shaping, adjusting, and evolving. It does not develop in a vacuum, as an internal mass of emotions or psychological construct; rather, it is constant and inseparable response to specific significant stimuli in the external world. Responses intensify into needs and become the essential motivating drive expressed primarily in the spine. Opposing influences exert their own driving force that bend and pull and push until they become the habitual, responses that are your character.

Dr. Dysart in Peter Schaffer's *Equus* characterizes the process this way:

> A child is born into a world of phenomena all equal in their power to enslave. It sniffs—it sucks—it strokes its eyes over the whole uncomfortable range. Suddenly one strikes. Why? Moments snap together like magnets, forging a chain of shackles. Why? I can trace them. I can even, with time, pull them apart again. But why at the start they were ever magnetized at

all—just those particular moments of experience and no others—I don't know. And nor does anyone else....These questions, these Whys, are fundamental....

Dramatic Characterization

As actors, you creates as fully-motivated and as honestly-responsive a human being as you are: Human beings with deep driving needs and desires, responding to forces that play against those motivating drives, with hopes that enforce and strengthen, with fears that conflict and resist; human beings with preoccupations and associations that play along with every immediate sensory response; people as fully human as any real human beings. On the other hand, actors create characters who exist to dramatize the motivating ideas behind the play; who will have only those traits, needs, and capacities for response that the story's themes require; beings created from a specific point of view who must function in harmony with all elements of the play in order to fulfill its total communication expectations.

A dramatic character, therefore, is a genuine human being who is also an artistic creation. Drama creates meaning and pattern from an otherwise meaningless, patternless life; it selects those essential traits that communicate an idea about life. This makes the dramatic character less complex, or at least more fully comprehensible, than the real human being. It also implies that the actor who would create a complete character, must fully comprehend the drama of which the character is only a part.

To create character in depth, actors must first create the world from which those human beings develop, the world determined by the concerns of the play. Actors should not think primarily in terms of psychological or intellectual or philosophical concepts; rather, they should think in terms of the interactive forces from which spring motivated spines and the patterns of natural habitual response that we call "character."

Who's Afraid of Virginia Woolf?

Because realism focuses drama principally on the complexities and changes of human character, I use it as a means of illustrating the process of characterization. Edward Albee's *Who's Afraid of Virginia Woolf?* dramatizes something about life in the academic world, which most students have experienced enough to be able to begin the work of creating the world.

In order to understand and to create the people of *Who's Afraid of Virginia Woolf?* we must create the academic world in which they live First, establish the interactive dynamics of the academy to expose the deeper thematic concerns and the animating forces of individual character motivation. Ask friends whose parents are administrators and teachers to help you set up improvisations to experience the determining forces behind the academic world:

- The need to establish one's self as a leader in the field

- Teaching versus research

- Departmental and school administrative responsibilities

- Sexual politics

- Attitude toward gender and sexuality

- The pressure of tenure requirements on new faculty

- The incursions made on a teacher's family and personal life by academic responsibilities.

At Theatre Arts U. the acting students attend departmental faculty meetings to begin their work on the world of *Who's Afraid of Virginia Woolf?* They assign themselves specific tasks: Find out what is important to the dramatic literature teacher. What does the playwrighting teacher want? What is the new acting teacher looking for? How do these motivations manifest themselves? Can you tell who was just hired? Who is up for promotion or tenure? What have become the determining factors?

Go to history department meetings and to the biology department. What issues compel these people, and how are they manifested?

Actors then create characterizations of the people they have observed with the perceptions they have gained. Improvise freely: Take the new teacher to the first faculty tea. Make the playwrighting teacher ask the directing teacher if he would like to team-teach a course next semester.

Observe faculty spouses. Do some active field research by babysitting for the department chairperson. Take a faculty husband grocery shopping where he meets the wife of the chairman of his wife's department. Become a new faculty wife and go to the opening reception for the new school year.

Make an appointment to meet with the Dean about some issue facing the school. Store up the administrator's spine and responses. When you are back in your room, improvise these responses until you can freely and habitually let them play themselves out. Remember your goal: to discover the why behind the how of behavior.

Assume the spine of your history professor and give a lecture to your class. Choose any topic you feel comfortable with, even if it has nothing to do with history. During office hours meet with a student about her grade on a paper, go home and mix a drink, or go for a run, or watch the news on TV, or read the paper, or walk the dog. Discover what is the most appropriate revelatory behavior. Perhaps this evening the wife of the chair of the history department attends a meeting of the Women's Board, or the husband of the chair of the biology department stays late at his own business meeting. You are analyzing the academic world in terms of improvised human behavior; that is, in actor's terms.

Read about the academic world. In recent years several books have appeared dealing with so-called "profscam." Read David Mamet's *Oleanna*. Go to the library and find the periodicals produced by various educational organizations. Look, for example, at what most of the articles in the AAUP publication concern themselves with. Take a look at the titles of the articles. Does this spark your imagination to create in terms of human beings in dynamic, illustrative interaction? Look for daily news items: an administrator of a university in Illinois was arrested for embezzling hundreds of thousands of dollars to pay for prostitutes at a suburban nightclub. Meanwhile, in universities around the country, financial aid moneys are being reduced. What kinds of currents emerge most influentially in small liberal arts colleges like the New Carthage of the play?

In some ways *Who's Afraid of Virginia Woolf?* has become a period piece. For example, why is it important that the play takes place in post-World War II America and before the pill changed sexual-social relations? How is this a significant influence? Gender issues play a significant part in the world of the play: The teachers are male; women are the spouses and that reality will influence the development of Martha's character. Sexual harassment has not yet become a volatile litigious issue.

Pay no real attention yet to the dialogue or even the particular characters. First, set up the world of the play and establish the major forces in terms of how they compete, conflict or support one another. The goal is to determine which currents carry people along in this world, which bend, strengthen, twist or collapse their spines. Work to set up contradictions and conflicting forces.

From all of the accumulated illustrations, let the play tell you which of the interactive forces that make up the academic world are specific to the world of *Who's Afraid of Virginia Woolf?* Set up, in terms of oppositions, in terms of real human beings in real human situations, the leitmotifs that run through the play:

• Personal creative curiosity versus tenure and promotion expectations

• Creative drives versus abortion or sterility (abortion of children, ideals, values.)

• Escapes (from what? Be specific.) into alcohol, sex, intellectual one-upmanship, wit

• What is the price of education? What values placed on education? How do we define happiness, and Love?

• In what is survival rooted?

• Male world of the academy as opposed to female needs, potentials, drives

• How is success measured? What are the ironies in this academic world of higher education?

• Procreation and creation versus What?

• The need to escape into imaginary worlds. Can you find the fragment of that in your own life? A student tells how she baby sits for one of the faculty members. Her boyfriend often visits. When did they start pretending the child was theirs? How did it happen? Why?

After you have created the determining currents that form the general network of the academic world, characters become specifically motivated by certain forces, or they reject others. Set up imaginative situations that can lead toward the development of specific characters. For George, create the spine of a young man who wants to teach. Improvise this young teaching spine:

• Give a lecture on your favorite topic.

• Go to the library to get the latest book you ordered for the woefully inadequate history holdings.

• Have cocktails with an older faculty member who talks about the days when he was his department's wunderkind.

• Meet the wife of the Dean in the pharmacy.

Add some oppositions:

• You are correcting papers and the Dean calls to ask you to serve on another committee.

• You are in conference with a student who loves history and the chairman decides to cut that class from the program.

• You meet the head librarian in the coffee shop and she tells you that the book you ordered was too esoteric and too expensive to buy.

• Find a passionately motivated young teacher (if you were such a teacher...?) What could happen to turn him into a George?

• Take him to the Dean's office with a new course proposal. The Dean says "no." What happens to your spine? Do you recover? If yes, keep improvising until the day comes when your spine simply hasn't the will to snap to and recover yet one more time. Start with such a moment in your own life when the power of someone in authority to squelch your enthusiasm was so strong that in fact your own spine was changed. (Every day a little death.)

What caused George's spine to collapse and never quite rebound? Find such a collapsed spine among the teachers in your own university. Note the slightly sardonic wit that often accompanies such a teacher's responses to his students: By what is it motivated? You are working to come to a muscle, sensory, and nerve comprehension of how someone becomes a George.

In the academic world, what specific stimuli does a Nick spine look for and respond to? Why does Albee make Nick a boxer? Let your muscle imagination play with the way a boxer looks at the world, responds to competition, makes his way, as opposed to a wrestler, a swimmer or a mountain climber.

What has become important to a Honey spine? Why? How did it happen? What forces play against that drive? Expressed how? in spine, voice, laugh, walk, responses to gravity. Note that it is Honey who insists that they accept Martha's invitation to visit after the party. Why?

Improvise significant biographical experiences (moments of realization and decision) in the Nick and Honey relationship. Be sure you state specifically what the experiential objective of each improvisation is.

For the developing Martha, create a world without a mother. Note that Daddy has a second wife. Set up administrative receptions and fundraisers. Perhaps the little girl of the house serves as hostess, constantly trying to please Daddy and never quite doing it. Perhaps Daddy calls her into his study to tell her how much he trusts her to be charming to the board of trustees tonight. Just as her spine relaxes and she feels comfortable with him, hoping for a hug, he reaches out and touches her nose and says lovingly, "Now you won't disappoint me as you usually do, will you?" Something within her winces, aches, longs to hear unqualified approval from him. She is becoming a Martha. Martha's love of and respect for her father and her obsessive need to please him become, through improvisation, experiential and developmental realities in terms of motivated spine and muscle and nerve needs. With these kinds of improvisations, the actor learns to create Martha through experiential realities rather than from abstract qualities she must somehow try to flesh out with a so-called emotional life. All too often that represents how the actor thinks the character feels about life experiences rather than an actual character responding to life experiences.

Actors work to discover why certain traits become intensified and others diminished, why one person is sustained by the same influence that threatens another. Two powerful sets of stimuli converge; a person must decide, not simply with intellect, but with the dynamic balance of active interests and forces at work within the self, which stimulus to accept or reject. Character is formed in the act of visceral deciding. A young man gradually becomes a George. A young woman begins to emerge as a Martha-in-the-making.

• Improvise the developing George and Martha relationship: Daddy asks a young Martha to show the campus to George, the prospective new teacher in the history department. What do they do? What qualities in each is the other attracted to from the beginning? Be actor specific. Explore, discover, and create in real experiential terms the deep positive bonds of love at the heart of the relationship between George and Martha. Without this foundation, the action of the play becomes simply emotional pyrotechnics, however engaging that may be.

Design your improvisations to lead directly towards a specific structural facet of the play:

• George is asked to come to the office his first day back from the honeymoon. "My boy, someday I want you to be chairman."

• George decides to read a book instead of go to Daddy's barbecue.

• George and Martha discover they'll never have children. When Daddy is told, what are the results?

• Improvise and discover how they came to create their own imaginary son.

• Discover through improvisation and observation how the gifts of love of language and ideas, intelligent and articulate minds, and wonderful verbal senses of humor, can turn to spiteful attack, ironic self-laceration, delight in the vulgar and the shocking in language. Do you begin to discover something about the irony of the value in American life.

• George and Martha get ready for a faculty party. Later you can get to, What makes the preparations for the party, and the party itself, unique to this evening? How are they responsible for the specific events of the play? Why is this the particular night when years of opposing forces finally come to a climax? For now, let George and Martha get ready for yet another of Daddy's cocktail parties. Your current objective is to discover how George and Martha have progressed, step by step, significant experience by significant experience, realization by determining realization, to become the people who will go to the party that will lead to the curtain that opens Act I on a situation that will forever alter the balance of all these forces and the nature of their lives. In the process, the play dramatizes, illuminates, communicates to an audience something about being human in the world of American higher education.

Character is not an entity separate from the play; it is a direct outgrowth and an embodiment of the forces that create the world of the play. Character emerges from a background of such forces. The objective of this work is to discover the motivated spine of a character as it emerges from the influence of these dynamic forces.

Working improvisationally on character creates a way of thinking that is the actor's point of view. Actors begin to account for the play's elements in terms of human interaction and behavior, not simply in terms of thematic or intellectual abstractions. Actors begin to see these elements in balanced and meaningful orchestration, rather than seeing only "my character" to the exclusion of all else. The more you read plays from an inherently dramatic point of view, as art that is forged directly from human behavior, the easier it becomes to see and hear what was imagined by the playwright.

• Do the same kind of work for Manet's *Oleanna*. Discover which forces of the contemporary academic world are most significant to the play.

THE WORLD OF THE PLAY: CHEKHOV'S RUSSIA
....

Following the process illustrated with *Who's Afraid of Virginia Woolf?* create the world of Chekhov. Consult books that describe nineteenth-century Russia and specifically the Russia of Chekhov.

Look at paintings and listen to contemporary music. Read Chekhov's letters, his and Turgenev's stories, memoirs of the times, and so on. Use the world to steep yourself in images that will touch off your creative imagination. Here are some areas that find their way into Chekhov's plays:

Occupations

- What was the state of education and schools?

- Compared with Europe, what was the state of medical practice and the technology of medicine?

- What was the military as a social class? What was Russia's military relationship with the world during the last decade of the nineteenth century?

- Peasant life comprised what kinds of specific experiences?

- The rising merchant class

- Government and bureaucracy

Social Strata:

- Smalltown life

- Landowners and country estate life

- Recreation and Culture

  1.) Music and Dance: Consider European influences in classical music together with folk song traditions (Easy switch from rousing major key to melancholy minor key and back).
  2.) Love of literature and storytelling: Pushkin, Gogol, Lermontov
  3.) Food and drink: Social ceremonies, the place of the samovar.

- The Intelligentsia: What exactly does this word refer to?

  1.) Influence of French culture and language

2.) The love of animated conversation (Note the absence of radio, television, stereo, etc.)

3.) Place in political life of the country.

- Transportation and travel within cities, in the provinces

  1.) Infrastructure
  2.) State of rail travel
  3.) Relationship with Europe.

- Relationships among the social classes

- The concept of the Russian superfluous man

- Family ties: Relationships among the generations

- Social occasions and rituals

- Eastern Orthodox religious practices, holy days

- Nature of the so-called Russian Soul.

Explore some of Chekhov's general themes:

- Love of life versus ignorance and pettiness

- Isolated individual surrounded by people he or she loves

- The passage of time

- The heart's aspirations versus life's inertia

- The need for productive work

- Loss.

Conduct whatever research is necessary to translate these and other ideas into illustrative improvisational behavior

The World of The Sea Gull

The people of *The Sea Gull* are carried along by the forces of the commercial theatre world. Their lives are determined by its conflicting currents. Research and create the particular forces of Chekhov's theatre world. Do some of those forces exist in current contemporary life? (If they don't, the play may no longer be worth producing.) Arkadina is lifted by the forces of personality worship, of ego, of money and narcissism, of sure-fire formula plays. She succeeds. She glitters through this world a star. She has been created by these forces and we, who support such theatre, are responsible. We reward narcissism, we reward stars rather than actors, personalities rather than artists. As Dorn says to Polina:

> If society does make a fuss over actors, treats them differently from, say shopkeepers—it's only right and natural. That's the pursuit of the ideal.

Trigorin has triumphed in the world of commercial writing. What have he and Arkadina had to give up in order to achieve such success?

Opposed to the commercial urban world is the world of the Russian country estate. Research it and create it.

From the sheltered security of the country world, Nina longs for the commercial theatre world. She soars from her placid lake and is caught in the whirlpool, thrown into the rapids of a world that eats up its personalities quickly, where youth and beauty are essential, where the ability to seduce an audience is prized over the ability to artistically illuminate lives.

Treplev wants to be an artist; he has the soul of a poet and may very well be a deeply gifted writer. But he comes clashing against the compelling forces of the popular theatre. Arkadina and Trigorin thrive in this world and have discovered the money-making formula. They will destroy the näive Treplevs and Ninas who tangle with them in such a world.

Discover improvisationally the underpinning forces of the world of commercial theatre and the country world of *The Sea Gull*. Do some work on the external stimuli that strengthen the spine of the commercially successful actor and writer versus the stimuli that the aspiring artist/poet spine needs for nurturing.

Move to the more specific circumstances from which each of the characters has emerged:

• Recreate the life from which Arkadina emerged triumphant. List the factors you want to account for.

• Create Treplev's development as an artist in the shadows.

• Chekhov lets us understand how a person becomes a Trigorin.

• Nina goes from star-struck youth to young adult facing the realities of life in "the real world."

Can you make a bit of the opposing forces that underpin this world and create the thematic threads of the play.

The Spirit of Improvisation

Creating Character through Improvisation

"Improvisation" is a catchword for which everyone has a slightly different definition. In this book improvisation means the actor's purposeful way of exploring the implications of any idea in terms of actual human behavior. Through a process of disciplined trial and error, improvisation can reduce the energy actors put into the act of trying (especially trying to do something right) and focus instead on the act of discovering and creating. As the primary way in which actors "think through" and test any idea about a play, improvisation encourages actors to explore responses freely.

Improvisation belongs in all phases of the actor's work:

• As part of discovering the principles of the creative process, which is the focus of this book

• As part of the discovery of the nature of drama and the specific dramas of individual playwrights

• As part of mastering the principles of style and audience communication

• As part of the process of casting a play into performance form in the rehearsal period.

You improvise to discover and to create character response to the world in which the character lives. You improvise to discover character motivation. You improvise so that your muscles "know" what, for example, motivates Trigorin (Use his description of his early days in Act II to help stimulate your thinking); so that your eyes "know" and see what his see; so that your spine, feet and smile understand in their terms. And you make discoveries while you work to create relationships among people, between people and objects, people and environments. You improvise with others to discover and to create the drama of conflicting motivations, the drama that happens when opposing wants and needs clash.

Any improvisational work should include the following elements:

- A particular person
- In a particular place
- At a particular time
- For a particular reason.

Start with an improvisation to activate your own motivated character spine (I assume that becoming an actor is important to you):

- Particular person: You

- Particular place: The lobby of a theatre (Be specific.)

- Particular time: One hour before an audition for your favorite play

- Particular reason: To go over your audition one last time.

If these elements strike you as artificial, use whatever examples more accurately describe you in a "characteristic" situation. But choose elements that focus on the process of stimulus and response to get your totality "thinking" in terms of your character in response to its environment.

Let me stress that this kind of work is designed to allow you to explore freely and to make discoveries from the point of view of your senses' capacity to perceive and respond. It is not simply to carry out ideas about action that your intellect has already decided. Set up an environment in such a way that it is allowed to happen to you rather than one in which you make yourself do what your intellect knows is the right thing to do.

For the moment, avoid creating artificially dramatic situations. For example, a friend comes in to tell you that your roommate has just taken five hundred sleeping pills; what will you do?

After you have explored the process through your own character, apply to dramatic characters. Improvisation focuses actors' work on exploring and discovering while letting the play guide them in that work. Allow improvisations to come from the play. Root your discovery and your creation in the realities of the play. Discover why the play includes each of its elements.

- Particular person: Nina

- Particular place: The lake (Specific sensory stimuli)

- Particular time: The beautiful sunny afternoon the day before Arkadina arrives for the summer

- Particular reason: To fantasize about becoming an actress. Or to wait for Treplev to come for one more rehearsal of his play.

Activate your character responses. Discover motivation as it is manifested in specific sensory response. Let Nina respond to significant stimuli in the play. Work until you have freed the soaring Nina spine, lifting up to that pink cloud in the sky, standing on tiptoe as you watch the dancing sun sparkle on the lake, taking the curtain call that makes your breath come fast and short.

Add a major opposition as the play suggests. For example, Nina runs to the lake on that sunny day to daydream: "I want to be a famous actress." Then add, "But I love the security of this lake. I want to float away on that pink cloud of fame and fortune but my father and stepmother won't let me fly even to the other side of the lake."

Creating Relationships through Improvisation

Start with yourself. Set up improvisations that activate and illustrate your relationship with your father, your lover, or your best friend, making sure that you include the four essentials listed above. Think, "If I had a five-minute situation that best illustrates each relationship...."

Move to Chekhov. Work on the relationship between Treplev and Sorin through improvisation. Let the play suggest animating situations: In Act I, Treplev walks to the little stage with Sorin on his arm. He combs Sorin's hair and adjusts Sorin's tie as they wait for the others to arrive. Sorin watches Treplev set up the chairs and fuss with the curtain as he asks about Arkadina and Trigorin. To de-emphasize the undercurrents that carry the drama, focus on creating the relationship implicit in the behavior between the two men. Improvise situations similar to that in Act I but without the specific undercurrents of that significant evening:

• Treplev goes into the kitchen with Sorin for a late afternoon bite to eat.

• Sorin falls asleep downstairs and Treplev comes to take him to his bedroom.

Work this way until you touch off in yourself the deep love that exists between these two and how that love expresses itself. Later you can move to the specific situation in the play to discover the vital new currents that carry the drama along.

• Design character-creating improvisations for Oswald and Mrs. Alving and then move to improvisations that explore creating their relationship.

• What kinds of improvised situations do you create to illustrate the Hamlet/Gertrude relationship? What clues does the play offer?

Do the same for these:

• Fiers and Gaev from *The Cherry Orchard*

• Morell and Proserpine of *Candida*

• Torvald and Krogstad (*A Doll House*)

• A good current play

Creating the Situation Implicit in a Drama Through Improvisation

Again, begin with yourself. Create improvisations speculating on the situational forces that constitute the central dynamics of your family. Take special note of how seemingly abstract concerns, psychological forces and unspoken conflicts must become embodied in terms of human interaction as the basis of drama. Come to view the situation from as objective a point of view as possible by asking, "If my mother created such illustrations, what would she use?"

What about your brother? What if a compassionate but objective observer gave examples?

Next, improvise to explore and discover the active forces that underlie the situation of a drama: In *The Cherry Orchard*, the impending sale of the cherry orchard acts as the determining force behind the behavior of all of the characters all of the time. How will you improvise to create the truth of that force in actual human responses rather than in disembodied metaphysical terms or hollow emotional terms?

 • Varya cleans up the house after everyone has gone to bed knowing that soon it will all be sold.

 • Gaev goes into the billiard room the evening before Lubov arrives.

 • Lopakhin goes out into the orchard to survey the site where he would build the summer homes.

Conduct similar work with these:

 • Hamlet has come home to a world where people sneak behind the arras to spy, where the rules of moral and political behavior change rapidly (How will you illustrate that idea?)

 • Discover and create improvisationally the situation that underlies the drama of *Ghosts*.

 • What are the dynamic forces underlying the situation of *Candida*? What happens during the course of Act I that throws these relatively well-balanced forces into conflict?

With the underlying situation of the play grounded in experiential improvisation, improvise to think through in actor's terms the determining forces of the immediate situation of any act or scene:

 • Improvise the elements that create the homecoming of Act I of *The Cherry Orchard*.

Take Varya through the day, cleaning the house, getting the rooms ready, giving instructions in the kitchen.

Take Gaev to the station to wait for Lubov. When was the train scheduled to arrive? How long were Gaev and the others at the station before the train actually arrived? Improvise the moment

Lubov and Anya get off the train. Put Lubov into the carriage and let it drive up the long road to the estate.

Lopakhin gets to the estate hours early. In this house he is out of place. Finally, having seen Gaev admire the books in this room, he takes a book out of the bookcase and soon falls asleep trying to read.

Eventually, improvise the actual homecoming that is dramatized in the first act, but allow yourselves to discover freely, to include responses to character and situation that are not dramatized. If a play text is the result of the playwright's writing and rewriting, then actors should also improvise and re-improvise as freely to arrive at the same end result.

• In the last scene of Act I of *Candida*, Marchbanks finds himself alone with Morell. Improvise the specific scene, even after the lines are learned, to discover the direct line of the drama, to discover the significant realizations and decisions that lead the characters forward toward the final curtain. Truly effective improvisational work is guided by the playwright and the play. Always improvise within the play. This does not mean to stay only with the dramatized situations, but let the play incite you. The play *Hedda Gabler* indicates how crucial to Hedda's present situation was the previous summer's party when Judge Brack's eye was elsewhere and Hedda accepted George Tesman's invitation to walk her home. To discover one of the major decisions that led Hedda to her present situation, improvise this party. Create the determining realities. For example, Hedda realizes she is twenty-nine; how young was the woman with whom Judge Brack left the party? What color was her hair?

Improvisations of the kind that put Hedda and Ophelia in an elevator just to see how clever the actors can be are not appropriate to this kind of work. Improvisation is meant as a working tool to get the human being experiencing vividly and truthfully the realities that go into the development of character, or relationship, or situation. You improvise in order to translate intellectual knowledge into experiential, behavioral knowledge.

The Characterization of Arkadina

With the work of creation of the world and the situation of the play in mind and body, let's turn to creating a characterization of Arkadina in *The Sea Gull.*

• Begin with some aspect of yourself that connects to a fundamental part of the character (not to be mistaken for turning the character into facets of yourself.) What touches off the star actress response in you? What stimuli turn your spine into a spine that craves the spotlight and center stage? Be specific. Start your creative work by improvising these stimuli so that the Arkadina-you can become activated. Try taking a curtain call after having played beautifully your most favorite role in all drama. This "you" is the you that Arkadina the character needs as her lifeblood if she is to come to life as Chekhov envisioned her.

Lift your spine out of your pelvis. Put your hands on your hips as you check yourself in the full-length mirror. Or instruct a dressmaker in the creating of the dress you will wear for your first entrance in your new play. Try it on, decide whether the neckline plunges enough. Spin in front of the mirror: Does the fabric fall beautifully? Is the waist tight enough? Do the lines show off your "teenage" figure? Let yourself take a curtain call so that the dress will move perfectly; use your hips and your bosom as you bow. Lean forward to seduce the rich man in the first row (Try to get a diamond delivered in a long-stemmed rose backstage), turn to exit and feel the folds of your dress twirl about you. You are caught by the applause and spin about to face the audience, letting them admire your tiny waist, your hips. (There is a moment in *All About Eve* in which Bette Davis as Margot Channing does this beautifully.) Then, catch roses tossed to you from the audience, throw a kiss.

Arkadina has a beautifully-trained voice. It runs up and down the scale in liquid, magical tones. She is always "on." She senses people in the room, knows they are looking at her. She is beautifully balanced as she moves, able to turn and laugh and charm at a moment's notice. In fact, her body is always ready for such 180-degree responses.

Try: Arkadina enters a room (a party? a lobby? a gathering of a few friends?). Where does she look? Does she stop in the door? What does she look for, what does she see, as she enters? What does she do in response? Do this until your spine is so motivated, until you naturally lift your head and turn your shoulder seductively in response to a complimentary remark, until your free responsive totality responds effortlessly, naturally as an Arkadina. Receive fans in your dressing room after the performance and sign autographs. Let the Arkadina-you visit a group of aspiring young actors who have gathered to hear you speak to them.

Devise your own improvisations. Whatever touches off effortlessly and naturally the celebrity in you is the Arkadina that could emerge in you. Let your total being explore the idea: Arkadina is a star. Arkadina charms and delights others, gathers them around her at her feet. Arkadina will do everything to keep herself at the center of attention, on top of her world. You are letting your totality explore an idea from the actor's point of view, letting your spine and your hands and your voice and your muscles come to their own understanding of the why behind the behavior. You are not yet performing or demonstrating or acting Arkadina. You are simply letting yourself come to discover the Arkadina you can be.

Do not simply remember a time when you felt the way you think Arkadina feels. Work to create essential human capacities as motivated responses to significant stimuli which intensify into the essential needs and desires that underlie and drive your totality: Motivation and spine instead of emotions and feelings. Take your whole self and turn it into the character through improvised responses that become needs, desires, even obsessions and preoccupations.

• Direct observation: Life studies. Visualize the character "out there," the spine doing what it does in response to the specific stimuli that activate it: Arkadina's forty-three-year-old actress spine lifted against gravity, beautifully aware of movement and grace, of its effect on others, always seeking the center of attention. You see her "out there" and you take your total self to her, you become that Arkadina by touching off in yourself something of you that responds as that Arkadina responds "out there." By training your eyes to see, your ears to hear, your muscles to sense kinesthetically, by storing up images, responses, action, you give yourself the capacity to ask questions of your senses, to train yourself to know how to go searching for life models.

In the seventies, a reasonably famous celebrity who had been a fifties starlet, visited our school. She was performing in a play in Chicago with a lesser-known actor. Two chairs were placed side by side for them on our small classroom stage. She and her leading man ("Jim") came down the aisle, she a step or two ahead of him. When she got to the chairs, she lifted one, placed it several feet in front of the other, and swirled into a sitting position smiling to everyone. The actor sat behind her. She was genial, charming, deeply interested in student questions. Her spine lifted out of her pelvis, leaned toward the students. She sparkled, she laughed, she listened, she told stories. She charmed everyone. Nothing fake but always "on."

One particular moment set the bells off within me and said, "Store this up for Arkadina." She was asked whether she had children. Only an instant's cloud passed over her features as the star celebrity had to make a sudden switch to motherhood. Her smile returned and she proudly mentioned her son, "Todd." Then momentary puzzlement crossed her face. She put one hand at her waist, lifted the other to refer behind her to "Jim," and leaned back toward him, keeping herself facing the students. Laughing as though to say, "Silly me," she asked, "Jim, how old is Todd?"

It was a brief moment in a delightful visit, but when perceived and stored up, it provided illustrative and devastating images for the motivation of Arkadina and for the Arkadina/Treplev relationship.

Roddy McDowall took two photos of Elizabeth Taylor which are posed exactly the same way. Of the one from the fifties, he says he dropped by to see her one day and she had her hair up in a towel. He took the picture. In her sixtieth year, they posed the same photo. It looks remarkably the same as the first, but took a lot of time and careful lighting to set up. Associate this with what Shamraev is referring to in Act IV when he says, "We all get old and fade with the elements, esteemed lady, but you, most honored lady, are still young...white dress, vivacity—grace."

Sometime in the early eighties a photo appeared of Taylor presenting Benny Goodman with an award at a ceremony honoring him. Guess who has all of the focus in the photo?

Treplev's statement that Arkadina really is a kind person who nurses the sick finds its reflection in the Elizabeth Taylor who has fought hard for AIDS awareness. All the while, however, she simply must be the center of attention. But, as with Arkadina, can she help it? Can we blame her? Is she wicked for demanding center stage wherever she goes?

Take note that by using life models, you can avoid the danger of simply putting on an Arkadina mask, acting the way you think Arkadina might, which is nothing more than shallow mimicry. Nor do you want to turn Arkadina into you by saying, "How would I act in this situation? What would I do in response to this stimuli?" which is the major criticism of Method actors. Rather, you see Arkadina out there (and life models help); you activate some essential part of yourself that empathizes with her and then that self steps into her and brings the visualized Arkadina to life by letting you/her respond to the stimuli that activate her. Life models give your imagination a specific "out there" to work toward.

- Imagination:

1. Study photos of Sarah Bernhardt. Read the famous essay by Bernard Shaw comparing Sarah Bernhardt and Eleonora Duse. Which one is closer to Arkadina? Turn his words into motivated behavior. What do your muscles, your senses, your histrionic sensibility, discover about being a nineteenth-century star?
2. Is there an appropriate painting or photograph of a nineteenth-century actress?
3. Metaphor:

Arkadina the ringmaster snaps her bullwhip even as she chats and smiles. (Arkadina will have her way.) This may help in discovering her relationship with each of the other characters.

Can you suggest an animal metaphor of the tabby cat/kitten nurse/Juliet kind to illustrate the Arkadina/Treplev relationship? Try one for Arkadina and Trigorin. Another for Arkadina and Sorin.

4. Novels: The character of Clarissa from P.D. James' *The Skull Beneath the Skin* offers clues to Arkadina:

.....the dominant figure was Clarissa Lisle. The immediate impression, whether by chance or design, was of a goddess of classical mythology with her attendants....Then Clarissa fluted a small cry of welcome, spread bat-wings of fluttering cotton and ran forward....Clarissa had floated on ahead waving her arms and producing a stream of doubtfully accurate information....

He had forgotten how Clarissa could take on an almost luminous beauty.... the grace with which she used her arms and body....she did manage to convey something of the high erotic excitement, the vulnerability and the rashness of a woman deeply in love....seduced by her charm....

Simon was apparently to entertain them with music after dinner and the distant sound of Chopin from the drawing-room where he was practicing was pleasantly restful and evocative of her schooldays....And why was Clarissa draping herself over the boy, ready to turn the pages? It wasn't as if she could read music. If this was to be the start of her usual system of alternate kindness and brutality she would end by driving the boy out of his wits as she had his father.

And then the music was broken. Clarissa stormed into the room from the terrace. Simon heard her and stopped playing in mid-bar. The two voices sang on for a few notes then broke off. Clarissa said: "I'll have enough of amateurs before the weekend's finished without you three adding to the boredom. I'm going to bed. Simon, it's time you called it a day. We'll go together; I want to see to your room. Cordelia, ring for Tolly will you and tell her I'm ready for her, then come up in fifteen minutes, I want to discuss arrangements for tomorrow. Ivo, you're drunk." She waited with a shiver of impatience until Ambrose had opened the door for her, then swept out...Roma said: "Black marks all round. We should have realized that we're here to applaud Clarissa's talent not to demonstrate our own."

Turn these descriptions into perceived realities that lead you to Arkadina.

• Take the actress-you directly into the stimuli and the situations that will begin to turn her into Arkadina in the play. Arkadina gets dressed for the evening house party that ends with Act I. Choose the dress, select the jewels, the perfume, check face lines in the mirror. Go to the kitchen to instruct the cook about the supper to be served after everyone attends Kostya's play. Greet Dr. Dorn when he arrives for the houseparty. Introduce him to Trigorin. He asks Kostya about the play. Arkadina tells theatre stories as people sit at her feet (It is important to her that people sit at her feet, applaud her, look in awe at her). She sings "Bird in a Gilded Cage" as Trigorin plays piano. (Notice that all of these play, the specific improvisations may not be part of what is actually dramatized, but they are all suggested and contained within the play.)

Arkadina must emerge imaginatively from the world of nineteenth-century Russia and the theatre of the times, a world of values expressed in attitudes toward sexuality, marriage and family; toward stardom and the public attitudes toward celebrity. Arkadina must become an actress of her time, a type more readily suggested today by the life, career and physicality of an Elizabeth Taylor than of a Meryl Streep or a Vanessa Redgrave. Elaborate on this statement.

Let yourself transfer the work imaginatively into the specifics of the play until you have turned yourself into an Arkadina. Not "until you have eliminated your self and tried to replace it with someone else," but until you have taken your total self, intensified some parts, de-emphasized others, re-arranged yet others, add still others, to become you if you were an Arkadina. Work improvisationally through specific sensory response to specific stimuli until you are responding with Arkadina's motivation, until you see with her eyes, until you hear what she hears, with her totally motivated ego spine.

Now illustrate each of the major characters of *The Sea Gull* using the preceding principles:

• Activate the "you" that the character most needs in order to come to motivated life.

• Look to life studies for motivated behavioral traits perceived with comprehension in totality.

• Imagination intensifies and assimilates the above: can you use metaphor or photos? Have you come across the character in reading?

• Take this work improvisationally into situations suggested by the play.

Now complete the work begun on *Who's Afraid of Virginia Woolf?* by applying these ideas to create full characterizations of Martha, George, Nick, Honey.

Characterization is a complex process. The major difference between using yourself as an example and using a character from a play is that you exist alone in your entirety, but the character from a play has been created from a particular point of view. Only those traits that are necessary for the character to fulfill a specific place in the overall plan of the drama are necessary. I have used two realistic dramas to illustrate the concepts involved because realism demands justifying the most complex characters. The ideas behind the illustrations apply to all forms of drama, even those in which characterization is at its simplest and the world the least realistic (A play in which actors play everything from background trees to tabletops, hopping in and out of simple characterizations in order to focus on a fable or a situation rather than on the intricacies of human character.) Learn to let the play guide your work process, even as the creative principles behind the process remain constant.

Further Whys and Hows

Thus I say to you whom nature prompts to pursue this art, if you wish to have a sound knowledge of the forms of objects begin with the details of them, and do not go on to the next step till you have the first well fixed in memory and in practice. And if you do otherwise you will throw away your time, or certainly greatly prolong your studies. And remember to acquire diligence rather than rigidity....Any master who should venture to boast that he could remember all the forms and effects of nature would certainly appear to me to be graced with extreme ignorance, inasmuch as these effects are infinite and our memory is not extensive enough to retain them.

—Leonardo Da Vinci
(notebooks)

The Actor's Journal

The major objectives described in this book:

• To train yourself to perceive the behavior of others meaningfully, and to store it vividly in your own being.

• To learn to discriminate between what is revelatory and what is superficial behavior.

• To learn to see characters in plays as real people responding to their environment and whose behavior you can study as meaningfully as you do real-life people.

• To take any obervation of people, or any idea about people or drama, and always to turn it into specific illustrative behavior.

Journals have served artists well for centuries. Read the journals of Leonardo Da Vinci, Ludwig van Beethoven, Anton Chekhov and Henrik Ibsen. Designers keep what they call their "morgues," in which they record, organize and store up images that they will refer to when they need stimuli to set their imaginations creating.

For the actor, the journal is an objective record of your daily work. It is an artist's notebook. You record in actor's terms (behavior, response, action) your discoveries about life and art. Writing things down can force you to clarify what you have learned, or realized, or discovered; it can also help you clarify what you still need to learn. How often I hear this student: "I went home last weekend and I learned so much about people and relationships." But when I ask for specifics, suddenly the brows knit up and then, "Well, I can't exactly say what, but I know I learned a lot."

Keep a journal. Put what you learn into words, put it out there objectively. Your journal is also a good conscience, a good Jiminy Cricket. If you have nothing of significance to write today then you have lost a day of work on your craft and your art.

Be very clear about what does and does not belong in this notebook: This is your work journal, your acting notebook. It is meant to be an objective record of each day's work. It is not a diary, nor is it intended for generalized thinking, however passionate, nor for emotional purgings. It uses words and pictures, but its focus is the actor's creative media. Make sure you stick to that. Personal reminiscences, long discussions about your girlfriend or boyfriend, essays about what theatre means to you, and so on, must be kept in a separate diary. If it does not apply to something specifically learned about art, about life, about drama; something that can be applied directly to specific characters, relationships, or situations in plays; to specific principles of behavior or of creativity that you are working on, then put the idea in another book.

• Begin with a solid, down-to-earth working definition of acting. Not pipedreams and warm effusions, but as simple, direct and literal a statement of what acting is as a bricklayer would make. Include the playwright and the audience in your definition.

• Choose some great character from a great play and detail exactly your unique contribution to the creation of that great role. What specific life experiences underpin your creation of Shakespeare's Hamlet, Ibsen's Hedda, Shaw's Candida?

• Keep these kinds of questions at the heart of your daily journal: What did you do today to discover more about people? About responses to life? About principles of art? about theatre? About the specific demands of acting?

When you make a discovery about someone, ask yourself, "How does this manifest itself in what this person does?" Let your muscles, your eyes, your hands discover for themselves what they can about that person because of this behavior. Let your senses inform your mind about the why behind the observed responses. As you train yourself to observe and to perceive, let your senses and muscles always be wide open to make the deeper discovery of the motivation behind the behavior. In life situations the actor asks "Why?" and "What if?"

1. Record each day your most vivid visual response. Record exactly what you saw. Record in specific detail of sensory and physical response what happened to you. What did your eyes do? Your spine? Your heartbeat?

2. What did you fail to see? Let yourself see the same thing, only become a painter... an airplane pilot... if you were old... if you were French, Indonesian.... Take things you know or can research in actual experiences. Set up a program to find out about things you don't know. Record your work in detail.

If you were your father? If you were a teacher? The current Prime Minister of Israel? A grounds and maintenance worker? An old person who won't die? Your acting teacher? Former Presidents Reagan or Bush? Or Clinton? Hamlet? Record resulting changes in perception and in your response to the stimuli, however subtle. If you were Macbeth? Treplev? Let yourself see what they see, what you see if you are....And actually do it. Avoid the easy intellectual grasp.

3. Record the new and altered perceptions. What happened to you this time? What are the differences from when you are just you? What did you see that you hadn't seen as you? Why? Always let your eyes, your muscles, your totality (not your rational brain) tell you why. Make a daily journal of your discoveries about people in life and about people in plays.

4. Work each day to develop your actor's sense of metaphor as an inroad toward comprehension. How do your observings of sea gulls help you to create Nina? Be specific. How does that photograph of the Shah of Iran in the last days of his regime lead you to Creon? Did you meet a person who reminded you of a bullfrog today? Record specifics. Can you locate him in drama?

To avoid being overwhelmed and to give some organization to your work, start perhaps by taking one week at a time for each sense: "This week I will concentrate my work on eyes and the sense of sight." The following week, turn to the sense of touch. Follow the same format for all the senses. Let the discussion in this book on each sense and area of response suggest daily tasks and actor's assignments you can work out for yourself.

5. It never ends. The infinite variety of human behavior is cast into theatrical form and we get the art of it all. But the stuff of it all is what we're after now.

• What did you learn today about the Norway of Ibsen from reading, or about Ibsen's people from music?

• What did you learn about art principles today from your study of paintings at the local museum?

• What did you learn today about life, people, or art? How did you learn it? Can you apply it to acting? Be specific. Perhaps you observe behavior that reminds you of a play you are studying: If your next-door neighbor's son treats his grandfather just as Treplev treats Sorin, describe what specific behavior reveals the Treplev-Sorin relationship. Improvise it to let your own behavior senses explore the idea; become comfortable with the responses, until you truly comprehend the why behind the behavior. Then apply to Treplev and Sorin. Record your discoveries in clear, detailed, active writing.

6. Voice and Movement

Acting communicates the experience of lives lived. It communicates in the specific ways of theatre, not just as an objective demonstration of those lives lived. Actors must be artists enough to be able to create, express and communicate any kind of experience from any human point of view to an audience.

Record each day what you did to develop specific elements of physical work for the actor:

• A spine that is supple, flexible, strong, responsive to every stimulus, capable of every motivational response to life.

• Muscles that are highly tuned, ready to respond with ease and with follow-through.

• Bodies that are balanced, coordinated (What does the word really mean?), ready for action; as expressive as a dancer, as strong and as responsive as a gymnast.

• Actors must learn to walk, talk, stand, sit and move in any manner that human beings are, or ever were, capable of. They must do it all as naturally, as habitually, and with as unconscious a comprehension as though they were born to it. They must do it with the communicative expressiveness of the great artists of movement and dance.

• Each day as part of your journal, record your response to questions such as these:

> What work did you do today to achieve balance, or
> a flexible responsive spine? Physically, what did you
> do to develop opposition and contradiction? With
> what results? What will you work on tomorrow as a
> result of today's discoveries? What are the next day's
> objectives?

Did you work on Richard III's physical distortions? What did you learn about body compensation, or about the importance of a flexible, responsive spine?

- Laura Wingfield from *The Glass Menagerie*
- Caliban from *The Tempest*.

c. Did you work to study the effects of gravity on the human body? What did you discover as a determinant of character, or of motivation? What specific work did you do? With what results? Start with yourself. Go to people you know. Lead to Solyony, Willie Loman, The Madwoman of Chaillot.

The actor must develop a voice that is capable of creating and communicating the total range of human vocal response to living. It means possessing a voice that responds to, and is the vocal extension of, any part of the human being. It must be wider in range, have greater depth, more variety of tone, more rhythm, a clearer understanding of pitch, meter and intonations. You must do it all with the communicative powers of a great opera star. Record each day what work you did to achieve these goals.

- The compelling minister's voice of the Reverend James Morell, a beautiful baritone that can lift long lines of Biblical prose and imagistic poetry up to the choir loft.

- Shakespeare's Cleopatra, whose voice changes over the course of the play from the willful, engaging tones and rhythms that enchant and madden Antony at the beginning, to the tragic heights of her description of Antony to Dolabella, and her stirring, "I have immortal longings in me" as she approaches death.

- Lopakhin's gruff, harsh, deep peasant voice, incapable of expressing whatever finer thoughts he might have, strangled and unable to say, "I love you" to Varya.

In the past decade or two much attention has been given to voice and movement. We have the theories and training of the Alexander technique, of Arthur Lessac, Cicely Berry, Kristin Linklatter; the physical focus of Growtowski in the seventies to Suzuki, Feldenkrais and others. Some teachers have developed their own methods by incorporating these and various other approaches. Take the trouble to find out what are the essential principles behind all good voice and movement training. Find a way to learn them. And get to work learning. Use your journal to record your progress.

> *I hear and I forget.*
> *I see and I remember.*
> *I do and I understand.*
>
> (Chinese Proverb.)

Concentration and Ensemble

For the professional athlete, concentration means a perfectly tuned body that responds on cue, without cognitive intellectual monitoring; a mind free to follow the body in reaching the goal, making the basket, the finish line, or the touchdown. Behind all of that freely responsive and perfectly disciplined being is the athlete's love of the game, the sheer joy in playing, and desire for the victory.

An athletic team works together. A team of basketball players are active, ready to receive the ball, eager to jump into play, even as any one player controls the ball. In one player's dribbling is the implicit promise of the pass as the other players maneuver, read signals, get ready for the pass and for the shot to make a basket. From sequence to sequence, their objective is to score a point or to block a point from being scored. They are educated in the requirements of the game: endurance and conditioning, dribbling, passing, shooting, the step-by-step process of certain plays, and so on. And they do it all with no tension whatsoever. As a group they are motivated to win the game. "Team play" is the sports world definition for the same phenomenon that "ensemble" describes for the performing arts.

In the world of music, the word "ensemble" indicates a group of musicians who have come together to play music. They discover the structural rules of each composer and each composition. They discover how each part contributes to a whole. They learn to find the throughline of the orchestral piece, to sense, to mark, to play the larger phrases and passages, to play measures, beats, sequences; to work together to create and communicate a totality to their audience.

Beyond character creation and personal moments and truthful response, actors must create the theatrical equivalent of team-playing. Something must happen to all the separate elements that creates an indivisible organic whole. Beyond perception, imagination, characterization; beyond relationships and situation; beyond all the personal and individual concerns the actor may have; beyond even dramatic conflict; beyond and beneath it all, the creation of ensemble demands the specific passionate and powerful concern for humanity that first fired the playwright to forge the play. Beyond their love of theatre and their great joy in communicating with an audience, actors must develop their capacity to extend their concerns beyond self, beyond their immediate environment, out to the rest of the human race.

Such passionate concern galvanizes actors who are members of the ensemble: to concentrate on the goal, to score the points, to "win" by sending home the play to an audience. The audience's gasps, or laughter, or tears, or applause, or utter thoughtful silence are the sure indications of landing the idea and scoring the point.

If an actor experiences great, truthful concern and that passion motivates all of his work on, for example, Creon from *Antigone*, it allows him to go from the individual realization, "The guilt is all mine...god help me, I admit it all," to suggest the deeper truth: "The guilt is ours...god help us, we admit it all." He may even communicate a contemporary concern such as: "We are destroying life on earth because we will not change the laws of commerce and industry that permit the destruction of our very planet."

Behind *Medea* is Euripides crying out against the deep injustice of an arbitrary law that reduces a princess to a barbarian, a non-entity. For today, it is the playwright crying out in righteous indignation against written or unwritten laws that devalue women in most arenas of the workplace; laws that exclude men and women from legal marriage because of their sexuality; laws spoken or unspoken that condemn people of color to the margins of society.

Actors in *Romeo and Juliet* must be capable of the deepest concern for the inevitable, sometimes tragic, collision between youth's drive to experience life and the adult world's instinctive need to put the brakes on.

To truly create *The Sea Gull*, the actors must care as much for youth caught in the destructive forces of commercial theatre as Chekhov did.

The powerful, animated current created by a group of actors whose shared concern is the human theme of the play demands more than shallow emotions or catchy technical effects, for that current is where the mystery of great drama begins and where the greatness of theatre resides.

How do people learn concern? How people's minds and eyes open to a world beyond them? Several years ago I saw a university production of *A Raisin in the Sun* acted by students, only a few of whom were studying theatre. The audience readily forgave the students their lack of theater expertise because their electric production was infused from its very center with genuine concern. Productions featuring theatre majors seem to be motivated too often by a desire to showcase or individual talent to prove that they should have been cast in last quarter's production. This group, however, formed an ensemble who had a purpose behind their playing, who were passionate in their need to communicate to their predominantly white upper-middle class audience something vital about the African-American experience. The effect of such ensemble motivation, of such immersion in the playing, was astonishing: It was real theatre. If they had been professional actors educated in the disciplines of their art, it would have been truly great theatre.

"How do you teach concern?" I wrote once to Alvina Krause. "You keep at it," she replied.

Interpretation

A play organizes itself around some thematic idea about being human that is as integral a part of the dramatic text as is the actual written dialogue. The thematic idea coupled with the playwright's point of view is the basis from which all elements of the play have been selected and organized. Together all the elements of a production of the play guide the actors in the process with interpretation. How these particular individuals, at this particular time in the life of their society, will be able to bring the idea of a play to life in the theatre is the essence of interpretation.

Stark Young writes in *The Theatre*:

> The sum of an idea consists in a set of relationships; its truth arises from the relation existing among its diverse elements.....A play is a piece of writing in which the idea has found a theatrical body for itself. The rightness of this theatrical body derives from the relations among its elements. But with the passage of time comes a change in certain elements; to produce the play again the relationship among them must be again discovered. To keep the play alive we must find always anew a body to express this idea. In sum we must translate it into the medium of the moment....If then, the fundamental problem in every revival of a play is how to restate it in such a way as to keep alive its characteristic idea, what shall we say of the type of revival that violates the quality of the play...? Well, that too is art. It differs from the intention of which I have been speaking in this respect: it does not aim to express the complete essential nature of the play, it uses the play to express some idea that the producer wishes to express...it is a sort of creation in which the artist takes the play as a theme or material from which to project his own special creation...know what your idea is that you either derive from the play or will employ the play to express. (pp. 92-93.)

We eagerly nod agreement with such statements as, "The mark of a great play is that it allows, even encourages, many interpretations," where "interpretation" means "my unique agenda," or "whatever I can do with this play that no one else has ever thought of doing." Young rightly says productions based on this thinking can be art, too. But it remains essential to learn the fundamental principles to "express the complete essential nature of the play" before going on to wrench great drama into expressions of their own personal visions of life. The teacher, I think, should teach first principles first.

Because directors may create any kind of interpretation they want, and because actors bring varying attitudes toward acting and the text, much of contemporary acting teaching proceeds upon the assumption that plays should mean whatever the actors or the director want them to mean. But plays do inherently mean something, and a playwright's vision should impress a singular shape on its production. The questions I ask assume that there is an idea of Lady Macbeth implicit in the play to help the actor in her search "out there" and "within her self" to create; there is an idea of a Candida that can serve as a model for the actor as a painter needs a model to paint, however personal the artist's vision may be.

Selective Bibliography

BOOKS

Allshouse, Robert, ed., *Photographs for the Tsar*, The Dial Press, 1980.

Boswell, James, *On the Profession of the Player*, London: E. Mathews & Marrot, Ltd., 1929

Cowart, Hamilton, Greenough, eds., *Georgia O'Keefe Art and Letters*, Boston.: The National Gallery of Art, Washington, in association with Bulfinch Press, 1987.

Fergusson, Francis, *The Idea of a Theatre*, Princeton University Press, 1949.

Gallwey, Timothy W., *The Inner Game of Tennis*, Random House, 1974.

Godine, David R., and Hillier, Bevis, *Victorian Studio Photographs*, 1976.

Hagen, Uta, *A Challenge for the Actor*, New York.: Macmillan, 1991.

———. *Respect for Acting*, New York.: Macmillan, 1973.

"Hume and Comedy," *American Theatre*, Vol. 8, No. 4., p. 30

Ickes, W., "Sex Role Influences in Dyadic Interaction: A Theoretical Model" in *Gender and Non–Verbal Behavior*, C. Mayo and N. Hanley, eds., New York: Springer-Verlag, 1981.

Johnston, Ollie and Thomas, Frank, *The Art of Disney Animation: The Illusion of Life*, Abbeville Press, 1981.

McAdams, Dan. P., *The Stories We Live By*, New York.: William Morrow Co., 1993.

Merker, Hannah, *Listening*, New York.: Harper Collins, 1994.

Mortimer, John, *In Character*, London.: Allen Lane, 1983.

Rockwood, Jerome, *Craftsmen of Dionysus*, New York.: Applause Books, 1993.

Rosenstein, Haydon, *Modern Acting, A Manual*, Sparrow, Samuel French, 1936.

Selden, Samuel, *The Stage in Action*, Southern Illinois University Press, 1941.

Shepard, Sam, "Silent Tongues," *Village Voice*, August 4, 1992.

Sullivan, Robert, "In Search of the Cure for AIDS," *Rolling Stone*, April 7, 1994.

Todd, Mabel, *The Thinking Body*, New York, London.: P.B. Hueber,Inc., 1937.

Young, Stark, *The Theatre*, George H. Doran Co., 1927.

One of the reasons for the unfortunate separation of acting training from interpreting dramas is that we hesitate to accept that there is a play there, that the play really does suggest strongly what it will always need Lady Macbeth to be. Is Lady Macbeth a sex kitten in her dealings with Macbeth or not? Does the play suggest that Candida manipulates the men in her life for spiteful pleasure, or does it suggest other objectives? How are we to know?

Chekhov's Nina is a sea gull; she is young and vital, alive to the world, "on tiptoe and with a fingertip touch to life" as Alvina Krause often described her. But each actress who portrays her will embody those qualities uniquely. If you have a young vital actress who can run in effortlessly on tiptoe, who has a grace and balance lovely to behold, and seemingly completely inborn, then terrific: that's Nina. If you have a Nina who is less adroit on her toes, whose sense of equilibrium is not simple and effortless, she will have to find some other way to embody the soaring, floating simplicity implied by the sea gull metaphor. But create it she must if she is to interpret the play that Chekhov wrote, if she is to play her part in the relationship among the parts that keeps the idea alive, as Stark Young suggests.

The principles that underpin the art of acting can serve as fundamental principles in an approach to dramatic criticism. Too much dramatic criticism is rooted too exclusively in ideas, developed theoretically, paying little, if any respect to the truths of the experiential. On the other hand criticism from the point of view of performance too often applies only to discussions of individual productions and is, as such, seen as separate from "dramatic criticism." If we recognize that drama exists principally in its embodiment in actual human behavior, then the actor's point of view on drama could be considered a central point of view for dramatic criticism. But that will not happen so long as acting teachers separate the principles of acting from the principles of interpretation.

Plays and playwrights should come back to center stage in acting education. It is artistic freedom, as well as an artist's responsibility, for actors to learn how to ask the questions of a play that can let it tell them what it needs of them. We can learn to ask a play to help us answer our questions.